CON...

see it p... ?

buy it p... ?

watch it entertainment | 28

taste it places to eat and drink | 38

know it practical information | 48

directory hotel listings and more | 56

speak it and **index** | 62

university of washington map | 64

Map references are denoted in the text by ❶ Greater Seattle ❷ Downtown Seattle ❸ Puget Sound ❹ University of Washington ❺ Around Seattle

seattle places to see

Wedged between waterways, framed by mountains, and painted with generous swaths of forest, Seattle is one of the nation's most scenic cities. The first American homesteaders arrived from Illinois in November 1851. They were greeted by a staggering bounty of natural resources—including seemingly infinite salmon runs and old-growth forests—and Suquamish and Duwamish tribes led by Chief Sealth, whose name was given to the new city. Since then, the famously overcast burg has become a hub of the aerospace industry, birthplace of the espresso coffee movement, and home of a vibrant indie-music scene. Today, Seattle is celebrated for its distinctive arts and entertainment venues, museums, restaurants, and markets.

see it places to see

Sights

Alki Beach Park ❶ 3B

On a sunny summer day, Alki Beach Park is the mecca to which Seattle's sun worshippers flock. In droves. If you dig the Malibu beach scene, Alki is for you. Young bucks can be found cruising Alki Avenue in souped-up low-riders while young ladies sunbathe; the beach volleyball courts are consistently packed; and the barbecue pits are perpetually smoking. And the views of Puget Sound, the downtown skyline, and the Olympic Mountains are absolutely captivating. *Free. Open daily 6 am–11 pm Apr 15–Oct 1, 4 am–11:30 pm Oct 2–Apr 14. 1702 Alki Ave SW, 206/684-4075, seattle.gov/parks*

Enjoying the Seattle skyline from Alki Beach Park

Boeing Future of Flight Aviation Center & Boeing Tour ❸

For aerospace buffs, there may be no attraction more exciting than this. The Boeing Company, which was created in Seattle in 1916, is the world's largest aircraft manufacturer. (It's also the country's largest exporter.) Visitors to the Future of Flight Aviation Center can revel in a 28,000-square-foot Avi- ation Gallery, with interactive exhibits, display aircraft, and time-lapse films of jet construction. The expanded tour includes a visit to the actual factory, where you can see 747s, 767s, 777s, and 787s being assembled. *Adm. Open daily 8:30–5:30, 8415 Paine Field Blvd, Everett, 25 miles north of downtown Seattle, 425/438-8100 or 888/467-4777, futureofflight.org*

Burke Museum of Natural History and Culture ❶ D1

Loaded with exhibits that cover the natural history and cultural heritage of Washington State and beyond, the Burke Museum, operated by the University of Washington, is a must-see for anyone (kids and adults alike) remotely interested in history, science, or botany. Recent exhibitions have covered everything from Mexico's Day of the Dead to the ongoing search for the giant squid. *Free first Thurs of the month. Open daily 10-5, until 8 pm first Thurs of the month. University of Washington Campus, corner of 17th Ave NE and NE 45th St, 206/543-7907, washington.edu/burkemuseum*

Discovery Park ① A1

The 354 acres of Discovery Park are a stunning blend of tidal beaches, sea cliffs, open meadows, dense forests, and sand dunes. Atop Magnolia Bluff, 6 miles northwest of Downtown, the park has views of Puget Sound and the Olympic and Cascade Mountains. It's also a great place for bird watching, beach walking, and sunsets. For runners and walkers, the park's 2.8-mile loop trail, which winds through forests and meadows, is a destination in and of itself. *Free. Open daily 6 am–11 pm, Visitor Center open Tues–Sun 8:30-5:00. 3801 W Government Way, 206/386-4236, seattle.gov/parks*

Experience Music Project and Science Fiction Museum and Hall of Fame ② D2

In a city with such a rich musical history and native musicians including Jimi Hendrix, Quincy Jones, Nirvana, and Pearl Jam, it only figures that its wealthiest rock fan—Microsoft co-founder Paul Allen—would build a sprawling temple to popular music. Inside the EMP, galleries display musical memorabilia that spans all genres of American pop, including hip-hop,

Boeing Future of Flight Aviation Center

Experience Music Project (EMP)

rock, jazz, and more. The interactive Sound Lab, which allows even the most musically challenged to learn the basics of guitar, drums, and bass, is a perennial favorite. Highlights of the Science Fiction Museum and Hall of Fame, within the EMP's swooping, Frank Gehry–designed building, include the original Darth Vader helmet and Captain Kirk's command chair.

Gas Works Park

Adm. Open daily 10-5. Seattle Center, 325 5th Ave N, 206/770-2700 or 877/367-7361, empsfm.org

Capitol Hill

Just east of Downtown, Capitol Hill is an eclectic mix of leafy parks, stately homes, and not-to-be-missed bistros, bars, clubs, and coffeehouses. Broadway between East Roy and East Madison Streets has long been the city's gay, lesbian, and transgender epicenter. Aside from a stroll along Broadway, top draws in the 'hood are the bars and restaurants on 15th Avenue E, quaint eateries on 19th Avenue E, and Madison Park, a wealthy residential enclave with one of the city's best lakefront parks. If time is short, grab a meal at Café Presse or Dinette, a drink at Smith, or a rock show at Neumo's or Chop Suey, or visit the Seattle Asian Art Museum in manicured Volunteer Park.

Frye Art Museum ❷ 4H

Bringing representational art to the people—without preconceptions—is the mission of this sleek, modern Capitol Hill museum. Past exhibitions have included collections of work by underground comic illustrator Robert Crumb, Leipzig paintings from the Rubell Family Collection, and manufactured-object assemblages by Willie Cole. The Gallery Café at the Frye is an ideal lunch or snack stop. Free. Open Tues–Sat 10–5, Sun 12–5, Thurs until 8 pm. 704 Terry Ave, 206/622-9250, fryeart.org

Gas Works Park ❶ 1C

Few public spaces in Seattle are more popular than Gas Works Park, on the north shore of Lake Union, which was once the site of a gasification plant operated by Seattle City Light. (The plant closed in 1956, but its infrastructure still remains; it's the only remaining gasification structure left in the United States.) On sun-soaked summer days, favored activities at this grassy, lakefront park include picnics, Frisbee, sunbathing, and bocce ball; it also has an outstanding view of

Downtown & the Waterfront

Downtown is the hub of Seattle's financial, retail, and cultural activities. The area is loaded with hotels, shops, restaurants, and associated attractions, including Pike Place Market, Westlake Center, and more. Pioneer Square, the oldest part of the city and Seattle's political and social center from 1852 until the early 20th century, sits directly south of Downtown. Today it is distinguished by Victorian Romanesque architecture and many art galleries. Seattle's 1.3-mile Alaskan Way waterfront promenade is a bustling mélange of working piers, ferry docks, marina space, and tourist traps. It's also an essential part of any visit to the city, for the views alone.

Downtown, 2 miles away. *Free. Open 4 am–11:30 pm. 2101 N Northlake Way, 206/684-4075, seattle.gov/parks*

Henry Art Gallery ① 1C

One of the city's most-prized artistic institutions, the Henry is tucked into a nook at the far western edge of the University of Washington campus. Founded in 1927 and the state's oldest public art gallery, it was radically remodeled in 1997 and is now a spacious shrine to contemporary art from around the world. The frequently changing exhibitions have included works by video artist Doug Aitken and photographer Alice Wheeler. Recent additions include the Skyspace, an innovative architectural/artistic sculpture designed by James Turrell. (Visitors actually enter the installation, a giant, egg-shaped chamber with a window open to the sky above.) The gallery also has a café and an outpost of Peter Miller Books. *Adm. Open Tues–Sun 11–5, open Thurs until 8 pm. University of Washington campus, corner of 15th Ave NE and NE 41st St, 206/543-2280, henryart.org*

Hiram M. Chittenden Locks ① 1A

This expansive complex of locks, completed in 1916, separates the fresh waters of Lake Washington from the salt waters of Puget Sound and is one of Seattle's prettiest urban parks. On Salmon Bay (between Ballard and Magnolia), the locks maintain the water level of Lake Washington, which is 20 to 22 feet above sea level. They also allow vessels to pass between the bodies of water. Visitors come to watch boats of all sizes passing through, and to see swarms of salmon migrating through the locks' fish ladder in summer and fall. *Free. Open daily 10–6 May–Sept, Thurs–Mon 10–4 Oct–Apr. NW 54th St, 206/783-7059, nws.usace.army.mil*

Myrtle Edwards Park ② 2C

A winding, 1.25-mile walking and cycling trail that runs along the shoreline is the centerpiece of this park on Elliott Bay, just north of the Waterfront piers. It's an amazing place to watch the sun set over the Olympic Mountains. The

Pacific Science Center

park is named for the late former president of the City Council and one of Seattle's most popular politicians. *Free. Open 24 hours. 3130 Alaskan Way W, 206/684-4075, seattle.gov/parks*

Olympic Sculpture Park ❷ 2C

This ultramodern outdoor sculpture garden, created and maintained by the Seattle Art Museum (SAM), opened to much hullabaloo in 2007. Its 2,200-foot, Z-shaped path connects three distinct parcels of land and winds through installations by preeminent modernist sculptors including Alexander Calder, Richard Serra, and Pedro Reyes. Visits most frequently begin at the PACCAR Pavilion (at the corner of Broad Street and Western Avenue), a glassy space with a café and indoor installations. From there, the path meanders down the hill toward Elliott Bay and Myrtle Edwards Park. *Free. Open daily, 30 min before sunrise– 30 min after sunset. 2901 Western Ave, 206/654-3100, seattleartmuseum.org*

Pacific Science Center ❸ 2D

It's quite possibly the most popular family attraction in the Seattle area,

Pike Place Market

and for good reason. In addition to highlights like a six-story-tall IMAX theater, the Willard Smith Planetarium, and the Laser Dome, where laser shows are set to the music of various popular musicians, the center has hundreds of hands-on exhibits and demonstrations covering everything from nanotechnology to tropical butterflies. *Adm. Open Mon–Fri 10–5, Sat– Sun 10–6. Seattle Center, 200 2nd Ave N, 206/443-2001, pacsci.org*

Pike Place Market ❹ 4E

Continuously operated since August 17, 1907, the Pike Place Public Market, on the western edge of Downtown just above the waterfront, is one of the country's oldest farmers' markets and the most iconic destination in the city. The market is loaded with produce, flowers, seafood, meats, poultry, breads, and cheeses, but it's also known for its wide selection of locally made arts and crafts and its vibrant

Fish vendor at Pike Place Market

street-performance scene. You can expect to see a number of musicians performing in the market's crowded halls and sidewalks on any given day. Some excellent restaurants, including Matt's in the Market and Café Campagne, are here as well. *Free. Open daily, hours vary by merchant. Pike Place, between Pike St and Virginia St, 206/682-7453, pikeplacemarket.org*

Seattle Aquarium ❷ 4E

For fans of salmon, sea otters, and starfish, there's no better destination. The aquarium has nine permanent exhibits, starring everything from harbor seals to six-gill sharks. A 2007 expansion added 18,000 square feet of exhibit space and a full-service café. But the undisputed highlight is the Window on Washington Waters, a 120,000-gallon tank with an angled, 40-foot-by-20-foot viewing window. With a wide selection of Washington marine life and a realistic design of rocks and kelp, it's easily the most arresting aquatic exhibit in the Pacific Northwest. *Adm. Open daily 9:30–5:00. Pier 59, 1483 Alaskan Way, 206/386-4300, seattleaquarium.org*

Seattle Art Museum (SAM) ❷ 4F

In the heart of Downtown, the Seattle Art Museum (SAM) is the city's artistic centerpiece. The museum was given a nearly $100 million refurbishment in 2006 and reopened to critical and popular acclaim in May 2007. Recent special exhibitions have included masterpieces of Asian art, paintings by Gaylen Hansen, and sculptural design pieces by Isamu Noguchi. Highlights of the permanent collection include modernist works by Warhol, Pollock, Lichtenstein, and Rauschenberg, as well as a vast array of Native American art. Perhaps the most arresting artwork on display: the 48-foot-tall, 26,000-pound "Hammering Man," a moving sculpture that stands on the corner of 1st Avenue and University Street, welcoming visitors to the museum. *Adm. Open Tues–Sun 10–5, open until 9 pm Thurs–Fri. 1300 1st Ave, 206/654-3100, seattleartmuseum.org*

Seattle Asian Art Museum and Volunteer Park ❶ 2C

Volunteer Park, which sits atop the crest of Capitol Hill, is an oasis of greenery amidst the chaos of the surrounding city. And the Seattle Asian Art Museum (SAAM), in the park, is an oasis within an oasis. The museum's striking, 1933 art-deco building was

Hammering Man sculpture

Asian Art Museum

home to the Seattle Art Museum until 1991. The SAAM's collection includes works from across Asia; recent exhibits featured Buddhist art, Japanese textiles, and Chinese art from a variety of dynasties. A pair of dromedary statues at the main entrance are great photo companions. *Adm. Open Tues–Sun 10–5, open until 9 pm Thurs. 1400 E Prospect St, 206/654-3100, seattle artmuseum.org*

Space Needle ❷ 1D

No single building better represents Seattle's pioneering spirit. Rising into the cloudy skyline like a giant-sized pin on some Herculean map, the Space Needle is the most ostentatious display of the city's technological and scientific ambition. And the view from the top simply can't be beat. The 605-foot-tall Needle, which sits on the Seattle Center campus, was built for the 1962 World's Fair, but it's anything but outdated. The birds-eye view can be had from the observation deck or the Sky City restaurant, whose dining area rotates 360 degrees per hour, ensuring a view from every angle during your meal. *Adm. Obser-*

Space Needle

Fremont & Ballard

Fremont and Ballard are two of Seattle's most rapidly - developing neighborhoods; both have eclectic mixes of trendsetting boutiques, stylish bars and restaurants, and old-Seattle architecture. Fremont's residents are notoriously humorous—in the early 1990s, they dubbed their 'hood the "Center of the Universe." Fremont, 4 miles north of Downtown, has a must-see sculpture: the massive, concrete Fremont Troll beneath the north end of the Aurora Bridge. It also has some top-notch shops and a host of excellent bars. Ballard, 2 miles west of Fremont, is best known for historic Ballard Avenue, a charming boulevard lined with excellent cafés, watering holes, and rock clubs.

vation Deck open Sun–Thurs 9 am–10 pm, Fri–Sat 9 am–midnight. 400 Broad St, 206/905-2100, spaceneedle.com

Fountain at the Seattle Center

Brilliant fall color

Washington Park Arboretum ❶ 2D

A botanist's paradise, this 230-acre urban park 2 miles northeast of Capitol Hill is home to over 20,000 plants. The park is most famous for its breathtaking azaleas, rhododendrons, pines, spruces, firs, cedars, and mountain ash, but there are a total of 4,600 different species of plants and trees throughout. Of particular interest is Azalea Way, a peaceful pathway bordered with the namesake flower. A winding path through the park and over waterways leads to Foster Island, an excellent bird-watching spot. The park was founded and is maintained by the UW Center for Urban Horticulture. *Free. Open daily dawn–dusk, Visitors Center open daily 10–4. 2300 Arboretum Dr E, 206/685-4725, depts.washington.edu/wpa*

Washington State Ferries at Pier 52
❷ 5E
Washington State has the nation's largest ferry system, operating 28 vessels on 10 routes throughout Puget Sound and the San Juan Islands. Ferries are an integral element of the region's economy, culture, and history. They're also one of the area's top visitor attractions, and rightly so—the view of downtown Seattle from the deck of a ferry is tough to beat. The best choice for a quick, enjoyable ride is the Bainbridge-bound boat; fares are only collected once for round-trip pedestrians. The sailing takes about 30 minutes, and the lovely hamlet of Bainbridge Island can keep you entertained for an hour or a day with restaurants, pubs, shops, bike rental outfits, and more. *Check Web site for fares and schedules. Pier 52, 801 Alaskan Way, 206/464-6400, wsdot.wa.gov/ferries*

The ferry offers outstanding views of the Seattle skyline.

Queen Anne
Directly north of Downtown, Queen Anne has some of the city's best restaurants, most lively clubs, and toniest homes. (In local parlance, Queen Anne is often divided into the homey and quaint "upper hill" and the more raucous and nightlife-friendly "lower hill.") Seattle Center, at the base of the hill, is an expansive urban park dotted with arts venues and attractions, including the Pacific Science Center, the Space Needle, and KeyArena, home to the NBA's Seattle SuperSonics. Magnolia, a wealthy neighborhood northwest of Queen Anne, is best known for Discovery Park, which is the city's largest public park and a must-see for nature lovers.

Ferry boat leaving the downtown harbor

Wing Luke Asian Art Museum ❷ 6H

Seattle's vibrant Asian community is well represented in this International District landmark, which displays artifacts, photographs, and exhibits from a variety of Asian Pacific cultures. (Permanent exhibits include "Camp Harmony D-4-44," a reconstruction of a WWII Asian-American internment camp, and "One Song Many Voices," which chronicles the 200-year story of immigration to Washington State by a variety of Asian Pacific cultures.) Named after Seattle politician Wing Luke (1925–1965), the first Asian-American elected official in the Pacific Northwest and vocal proponent of racial equality, the museum also hosts many community events, performances, and children's programs. In 2008 the museum moved into an expanded space. *Adm. Open Tues–Fri 11:00–4:30, Sat–Sun 12–4. 719 S King St, 206/623-5124, wingluke.org*

Woodland Park Zoo ❶ 1C

A favorite attraction of Seattleites and visitors alike—with the largest member base of any Puget Sound–area attraction or museum—Woodland Park is one of the oldest zoos on the West Coast, in operation since 1899. Today the zoo has more than 1,100 animals representing almost 300 species—including 35 endangered and 5 threatened species. Perennially popular exhibits include the Northern Trail, complete with wolves, arctic foxes, and brown bears, and Tropical Asia, whose elephant forest is home to

four Asian elephants and one African elephant. *Adm. Open daily 9:30–4:00 Oct–Apr, 9:30–6:00 May–Sept. 601 N 59th St, 206/684-4800, zoo.org*

You will find majestic lions and meandering peacocks at Seattle's Woodland Park Zoo.

University District

This neighborhood 5 miles northeast of downtown takes its name from the University of Washington (UW), whose sprawling, picturesque campus is the centerpiece of the area. The school is bordered on the west by "The Ave"—aka University Way NE—lined by retro boutiques, noodle shops, bookstores, and museums, a microcosm of eccentric, carefree amenities of college life. The U-District's top draws include the Henry Art Gallery, one of the city's finest, and Thai Thom, a hole-in-the-wall Thai eatery that draws crowds from across Seattle. Also here is University Village, a popular and luxurious outdoor shopping mall.

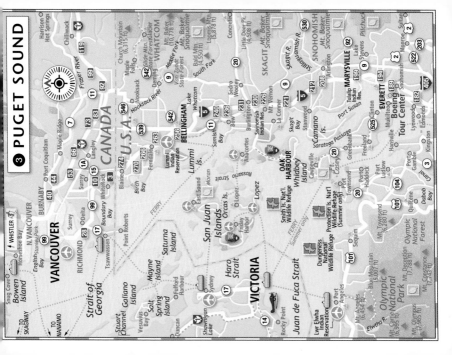

❸ PUGET SOUND

seattle places to shop

First-time visitors to Seattle often expect a sartorial sea of flannel and ripped jeans. But the city has come a long way since the days of grunge rock and drip coffee (circa 1991). Today Seattle's many neighborhoods are booming with trendy boutiques, vintage clothiers, independent book and music shops, and design/furniture enclaves. Downtown is well stocked with department stores, high-end fashion houses, and various retailers that cater to tourists. Yet some of the city's best shopping lies in Seattle's funky satellite neighborhoods. Ballard and Fremont are rife with independent clothing and housewares stores and accessories shops; the University District's retro-clothing outlets are its claim to fame; and Capitol Hill excels in books and music.

buy it places to shop

Shopping Areas

Ballard ❶ 1B

Ballard's brick façades and historic feel make it ideal for pedestrianism. The main shopping drag, Ballard Avenue, has an indie/crafty vibe, with many light-filled storefronts dating to the early 1900s—the best stretch is between 20th Avenue NW and NW Market Street, with everything from

Funky fashion on Capitol Hill

ultramodern shoes at re-souL to vintage furniture at Collective (❶ 1B *5323 Ballard Ave NW, 206/782-1900, collectiveinballard.com*).

Belltown ❷ 2D

Moneyed and modern Belltown, a mile north of Downtown, is a hotbed for high fashion. The once-downtrodden district now has loads of fine restaurants, crowded clubs, new high-rise condos, and small boutiques dealing in high-end designers. Top among Belltown's shops: Kuhlman, one of the city's best menswear dealers, and Macrina, a bakery not to be missed—at any cost.

Capitol Hill ❶ 2C

The stylish twenty-somethings trolling Capitol Hill's streets seem to have been pulled from the pages of the latest fashion rag. Here, in the center of Seattle's hipster universe, indie clothiers, record shops, design stores, and vintage retailers abound. Some places to start: Atlas Clothing and Red Light (for vintage duds); and Broadway Market (for Urban Outfitters).

Downtown ❶ 2B

In the city that begat Nordstrom—the department store empire was launched here in 1901—there are more than a few high-end fashion institutions. And, with rare exceptions, they can all be found Downtown. From Barney's to Nordstrom to Mario's (❷ 3F *1513 6th Ave, 206/223-1461, marios.com*), the wealth of lavish retailers could exhaust even the most die-hard dilettante.

Fremont ❶ 1B

Seattle's quirkiest (and perhaps most charming) neighborhood harbors indie retailers of all stripes, and its smallish size is well suited to strolling in pursuit of one-of-a-kind finds, from handmade greeting cards to rustic frocks. Head to Les Amis for that singular dress and for eclectic gifts, cards, and ornaments, stop by Portage Bay Goods (❶ 1C *706 N 34th St, 206/547-5221, portagebaygoods.com*).

University District ❶ 1C

Most of the city's best vintage and retro shops are on University Way NE, i.e., "The Ave," where you can scour the racks for pearl-buttoned cowboy shirts and vintage jeans at top-notch shops such as Red Light and Buffalo Exchange. The Ave also has a wealth of boutiques with new clothing and shoes and second-hand books and music.

Books & Music

Bailey/Coy Books ❷ 1H

One of Seattle's finer independent bookstores, and a Capitol Hill institution, Bailey/Coy is known for its outstanding service. Customers often walk in with only a vague idea of what they're looking for, and walk out with an armful of standout titles. *414 Broadway E, 206/323-8842, bailey coybooks.com*

Easy Street Records ❷ 1C

Looking for that late-60s R&B classic, on vinyl? Easy Street's got it—along with virtually every other genre of music. The lower Queen Anne store has an incredible selection of used and new CDs and vinyl, plus live, in-store concerts on an almost weekly basis. *20 W Mercer St, 206/691-3279.*

Also: 4559 California Ave SW, 206/938-3279. easystreetonline.com

Elliott Bay Book Company ❷ 5A

This Pioneer Square bookstore is housed in the Globe Building, which has presided over the intersection of First Avenue and South Main since 1890. The creaking floors, soaring ceilings, and exposed brick walls evidence the building's age, but the store's 150,000 titles are anything but antiquated. *101 S Main St, 206/624-6600, elliottbaybook.com*

Vintage vinyl

Sonic Boom Records ❶ 1B

It's small in size, but there's more rock and roll per square foot in this vibrant shop than anywhere else in Seattle. The specialty is local indie rock, but you can pick up the latest pop, soul, or hip-hop release before grabbing one of the store's signature t-shirts. *2209 NW Market St., 206/297-2666. Also: 514 15th Ave E, 206/568-2666. sonicboomrecords.com*

Twice-Sold Tales ❷ 2H

The name says it all: there's no better place to find a used book than this Capitol Hill bookshop. The store is well-known for its wide selection of used books (both fiction and nonfiction) and for its population of cats, which lounge about as if they owned the place. *905 E John St, 206/324-2421*

University Bookstore ❹

A vast shrine to the written word, the University Bookstore is the go-to store for that rare title, distinctive coffee-table book, or University of Washington (UW) sweatshirt. (The store has a large collection of UW swag.) Parking is free with validation, and there's an extensive selection of pens and stationery. *4326 University Way NE, 206/634-3100, bookstore.washington.edu*

Clothes & Accessories

Anthropologie ❷ 3F
Seattlleites aren't immune to the overtures of this more sophisticated, more expensive, and more feminine sister chain to Urban Outfitters. Its whimsical, mid-century-retro take on women's apparel and furnishings is formulaic but dependable, especially for boho-chic dresses, nighties, and costume jewelry. *1509 5th Ave, 206/381-5900, anthropologie.com*

Blackbird ❶ 1B
Thanks to clothiers like Blackbird, Seattle men are finally abandoning flannel and fleece. Favored by the young, stylish, and successful, this shop just off Ballard Avenue stocks brands like APC, Robert Geller, and RVCA. Austere, slim-fitting outerwear and jeans, polished shoes, sunglasses,

and fedoras steal the show. *5410 22nd Ave NW, 206/547-2524, helloblackbird.blogspot.com*

Kuhlman ❷ 3D
This swanky men's high-fashion hangout in the heart of Belltown has excellent service and a wide selection of contemporary clothing for the slightly edgy urban man. Jeans are fashion-forward and authentically distressed; tees are obscure and artsy; suits are smart and slim. There's a limited

Fashionable Seattle

women's selection, too. *2419 1st Ave, 206/441-1999*

Les Amis ❶ 1C
A favorite of well-dressed women from Madison Park to Ballard, this Fremont boutique is stocked with fine frocks, jewelry, and lingerie. Featured designers include Rozae Nichols, Trina Turk, and Diane Von Furstenberg. If you need a sassy, simple party dress, this is your place. *Closed Mon. 3420 Evanston Ave N, 206/632-2877, lesamis-inc.com*

MoMo ❷ 6G

A lovely little boutique that opened in 2007, Momo is the first high-fashion store to arrive in the International District. The shop is loaded with simple, subdued men's and women's fashions—olive, gray, and black are the most common colors here, with high-style jeans by True Brit, and French fashions by Cop Copine—and the jewelry is handmade and local. *600 S Jackson St, 206/329-4736, momoseattle.com*

Olivine ❶ 1B

Created in the truest French style—there's even a dog in residence—this Ballard boutique has a selection of casual and semiformal dresses sometimes criticized for appealing mainly to Audrey Hepburn–size francophiles, but the denim, shoes, cosmetics, and jewelry are top-notch as well. *5344 Ballard Ave NW, 206/706-4188, olivine.net*

Undies and Outies/Queen Anne Mail & Dispatch ❶ 2B

A unique combination of women's clothing and a mom-and-pop shipping service, this neighborhood mainstay is a hodgepodge of denim, blouses, and lingerie catering mainly to twenty-somethings. But there's also a wide array of cards, shoes, accessories, and stamps. Regulars rave about the sales. *2212 Queen Anne Ave N, 206/286-1024, undiesandouties .com*

Department Stores

Barneys New York ❶ 4F

With a well-deserved reputation for the finest au courant clothing, Barneys attracts a stylish and moneyed clientele who appreciate chic, urbane fashions. Departments include formal and semiformal menswear; sophisticated women's dresses, jackets, and denim; and a selection of casual and formal shoes for both sexes. *1420 5th Ave, #110, 206/622-6300. Also: 600 Pine St, 206/622-6300. barneys.com*

Macy's ❷ 3F

One of just two major department stores downtown (Nordstrom being

Boutiques Galore

Seattle is known for its independent spirit and true to form, Seattleites frequently eschew big-box retailers in favor of locally owned boutiques, restaurants, and cafés. The best of Seattle's boutiques include MoMo, Olivine, Kuhlman, and Undies and Outies. Other boutiques of note: Fremont's adorable Frock Shop (*6500 Phinney Ave N, 206/297-1638, shopfrock shop.com*); Hitchcock, a Madrona gem specializing in handbags and jewelry (❷ 3D *1406 34th Ave, 206/838-7173, shophitchcock.com*); La Rousse, a fashion-forward downtown enclave (❷ 3E *430 Virginia St, 206/448-1515, la-rousse.com*); and Merge, a Ballard boutique with young, hip fashions (❶ 1C *611 N 35th St, 206/782-5335, mergeboutique .blogspot.com*).

the other), Macy's offers a bit of everything: fine women's fashions (Anne Klein, Ralph Lauren, Michael Kors), lingerie, cosmetics, mattresses, and menswear. The massive store also has a large selection of handbags, accessories, and children's clothing. *1601 3rd Ave, 206/506-6000, macys.com*

Nordstrom ❷ 3F

In 1901 Swedish immigrant John W. Nordstrom opened a shoe store in downtown Seattle. In the 108 years since, the Nordstrom family has built the company into an upscale department store empire, with 101 stores as of 2008. The downtown Seattle flagship store is a shopper's Valhalla. *500 Pine St, 206/628-2111, nordstrom.com*

Food & Wine

DeLaurenti ❷ 4F

Nestled into a nook at the south end of the Pike Place Market, DeLaurenti has a wide selection of specialty groceries and wines. The inventory includes an entire wall of olive oil and a seemingly endless supply of chocolates. The deli—which makes excellent paninis and pizzas—stocks over 250 artisan cheeses from around the world. *1435 1st Ave, 206/622-0141, delaurenti.com*

Esquin Wine Merchants ❶ 4C

Seattle's largest wine shop stocks over 4,000 labels. Just south of Safeco Field in SoDo (South of Downtown), Esquin has been serving Seattle wine aficionados since 1969, and its certified sommeliers can help you find the perfect bottle for any occasion. On Thursday and Saturday the store has

The perfect bottle

complimentary tastings. *2700 4th Ave S, 206/682-7374, esquin.com*

Uwajimaya ❷ 6G

First opened in Tacoma in 1928 and relocated to Seattle after World War II, Uwajimaya has a selection of Asian foods and accessories unrivaled in the Pacific Northwest. A visit should be a required element of any tour of the International District. *600 5th Ave S, 206/624-6248, uwajimaya.com*

Furniture & Design

Design Within Reach ❷ 2E

Mass-production of classic mid-century-modern pieces such as the famed Mies van der Rohe Barcelona chair and Saarinen Pedestal Table is the raison d'être of Design Within Reach, which has nearly 70 outlets across North America. Just 2 blocks east of the Pike Place Market, it is stocked with designs for the home and office, including lighting, accessories, outdoor furniture, and floor coverings. *1918 First Ave, 206/443-9900, dwr.com*

Elegant home accents

Kasala ❷ 4E
A high-end retailer of modern-traditional home furnishings, Kasala has earned a reputation as one of Seattle's best furniture sources. The store, which is one block east of the waterfront, is stocked with sofas and armchairs—many in leather—Lucite tables, angular dark-wood beds, and more, by designers such as Baronet, Natuzzi, and Alessi. *1505 Western Ave, 206/623-7795, kasala.com*

McKinnon Furniture ❷ 5E
All of the contemporary hardwood furniture at McKinnon is handcrafted by expert woodworkers, making each piece unique. One block east of the waterfront, the store also provides consulting and does custom work. *1201 Western Ave, #100, 206/622-6474, mckinnonfurniture.com*

Gifts & Souvenirs

Archie McPhee & Co. ❶ 1A
Come for the Bacon Strip Bandages, stay for the Avenging Narwhal Play Set. With an inventory ranging from the kooky (e.g., the Gummy Haggis) to downright outrageous (e.g., the Yodeling Pickle), Archie McPhee, in the heart of Ballard, is far and away the city's most entertaining toy-and-novelty store. *2428 NW Market St, 206/297-0240, mcphee.com*

Clutch ❷ 4F
The city's only handbag boutique, diminutive and adorable Clutch features a leather rainbow of totes, purses, and clutches from independent designers such as Botkier, Goldenbleu, and Rebecca Minkoff. *At the Fairmont Olympic Hotel, 1212 4th Ave, 206/624-2362, clutchseattle.com*

Peter Miller ❷ 4E
In a historic storefront on First Avenue, just above the Pike Place Market, Peter Miller sells a variety of architecture and design books, office and stationery products, and various design accessories. It's not to be missed by architects, designers, or anyone with a serious sense of style. *Closed Sun. 1930 1st Ave, 206/441-4114, petermiller.com*

re-souL ❶ 1B
Ballard's chief arbiter of style, re-souL carries fashionable footwear, trendy accessories, jewelry, and home furnishings. The shoe selection runs from sleek, leather men's boots by Cydwoq to retro-inspired women's platforms by Biviel. Accessories include colorful handbags by Astrosatchel, and the store also sells locally made modern furnishings by Kerf Design. *5319 Ballard Ave NW, 206/789-7312, resoul.com*

Malls

Broadway Market ❷ 1H
Worth visiting if you're strolling the length of Broadway, this mall is home

to several clothing stores—including Urban Outfitters—a selection of small arts and crafts dealers, a number of restaurants, and even a grocery store. *401 Broadway E, 206/322-1610*

Pacific Place ❷ 3F

The Downtown cousin of University Village, Pacific Place is a multilevel mall that's loaded with a similar selection of luxury stores and the poshest in chain retail—including Barney's, Cartier, Benetton, and Coach. And, in case one tires of shopping, an 11-screen multiplex is located on the top two floors. *600 Pine St, 206/405-2655, pacificplaceseattle.com*

University Village ❶ 1D

The largest open-air mall in Seattle, exquisitely designed University Village is home to upscale retailers such as Anthropologie, the North Face, the Apple store, and Restoration Hardware. Restaurants and cafés include Pasta & Company, Blue C Sushi, and the ubiquitous Starbucks. *2600 NE University Village, 206/523-0622, uvillage.com*

Markets

Pike Place Market ❷ 3E

Founded in 1907 by city councilman Thomas Revelle in response to price-gouging grocers, the Pike Place Market has grown into one of the nation's best markets, with unbeatable selections of produce, meats, cheeses, and arts and crafts. It's the daily destination of 120 farmers and 190 craftspeople, and attracts 10 million visitors each year. *Many merchants are cash only. 1531 Western Ave, 206/682-7453, pikeplacemarket.org*

Fresh crab at Pike Place Market

University District Farmer's Market ❶ 1C

The largest and most popular of Seattle's many weekly neighborhood markets, this is an ideal Saturday morning

Outdoor Gear

Despite its relative dearth of sunshine, Seattle is home to an impressively active citizenry, and a number of first-rate outdoor equipment manufacturers and retailers meet the demand. Most famous among these is REI, whose flagship store draws hikers, climbers, bikers, and kayakers from far and wide. Hard-core alpinists should not miss Feathered Friends (❷ 2G *119 Yale Ave N, 206/292-6292, featheredfriends.com*), a downtown climber's shop that's been in business since 1972. Traditional outdoorsmen and women appreciate the gently anachronistic designs of C.C. Filson Co., which has been operating in Seattle since 1897.

destination. Fresh wild salmon, free-range eggs, and locally grown vegetables, beef, and chicken are the most sought-after items. It's open on Saturday only. *No credit cards. Corner of NE 50th St and University Way NE, seattlefarmersmarkets.org*

Sporting Goods

C.C. Filson Co. ● 5C
This manufacturer of rugged outdoor clothing was founded in 1897; since then Filson has produced high-end jackets, work wear, and hunting clothing for generations of American sportsmen. The company's flagship store, in SoDo (South of Downtown), is a paradise for hunters, anglers, and outdoors lovers of all stripes. *1555 4th Ave S, 206/622-3147, www.filson.com*

Patagonia ● 3E
Smart, well-built outdoor clothing for eco-conscious consumers is the hallmark of this brand. The fleece jackets, for one, are made from recycled plastics, and much of the cotton clothing is organic. The Belltown outlet has a knowledgeable and friendly staff, and some of the best-wearing clothing on the market. *2100 1st Ave, 206/622-9700, patagonia.com*

REI ● 2G
Founded in Seattle in 1938, Recreational Equipment Incorporated has grown into the nation's largest consumer cooperative, with over three million members. The flagship store, at the base of Capitol Hill, is also the nexus of Seattle's outdoor recreation scene. Attractions include a 65-foot climbing wall, a mountain-bike test trail, and a treasure trove of outdoor gear. *222 Yale Ave N, 206/223-1844, rei.com*

Vintage Clothes

Atlas Clothing ● 3H
The best of the thrift store experience, Atlas stocks quality men's and women's vintage clothing that you don't have to sift through endless racks of hopelessly uncool duds to find. The store buys and sells only the most fashionable clothing, yet prices remain reasonable. *1515 Broadway, 206/323-0960, atlasclothing.net*

Buffalo Exchange ● 1C
A longtime University District standby for vintage hounds, Buffalo Exchange is part of an expanding empire (with 33 stores in 13 states), but maintains its intimate, independent feel. And the clothing remains as hip and fun as it ever was. *4530 University Way NE, 206/545-0175, buffaloexchange.com*

Red Light ● 1C
Just a few doors up "the Ave" from Buffalo Exchange, Red Light has built its reputation on quality used clothing that's stylish and always current. Seattle's largest vintage store is a delightful mélange of contemporary and retro: name-brand designs and retro skirts, jeans, and accessories. *4560 University Way NE, 206/545-4044. Also: 312 Broadway E, 206/329-2200. redlightvintage.com*

seattle entertainment

Seattle's long-revered, rollicking music scene continues to flourish, but today's entertainment culture encompasses much more than just indie rock. A bustling theater community has grown in popularity; the Seattle Symphony is evolving into one of the nation's finest; the dance scene is thriving, thanks in part to the success of the Pacific Northwest Ballet; and the city's major sports teams garner healthy crowds. Popular annual music and arts festivals include the Northwest Folklife Festival *(206/684-7300, nwfolklife.org)*, Bumbershoot *(206/281-7788, bumbershoot.org)*, and the Earshot Jazz Festival *(206/547-6763, earshot.org)* in late October.

watch it entertainment

Tickets

The online ticket agencies listed below are your resources for tickets that aren't available directly from box offices.

Ticketmaster ❷ 3F

The grande dame of ticket agencies brokers tickets for most of the city's large concerts and sports events. *Westlake Center, 400 Pine St, ticketmaster.com*

Space Needle

Ticketweb

Specializes in live music ticket sales; many of the city's mid-size rock clubs use this service to sell event tickets online. *866/468-7263, ticketweb.com*

TicketsWest

Deals in local arts, music, and sporting events. *800/992-8499, ticketswest.com*

Performing Arts Centers

Paramount Theatre ❷ 3G

As Seattle's preeminent theater, the Paramount hosts big-name national and international musicians, performance artists, speakers, and comics. Built in 1928, the theater is ornate and striking; its coved ceiling, expansive balcony, and opulent lobby set it apart from any other venue in Seattle. *911 Pine St, 206/467-5510, the paramount.com*

Town Hall ❷ 4G

On the eastern edge of Downtown, Town Hall hosts a wide variety of musical and cultural events in a fully restored Roman-revival-style building. It's the site of an increasing number of chamber-music performers, including the Northwest Sinfonietta and the Octava Chamber Orchestra. *1119 8th Ave, 206/654-4255, townhallseattle.org*

Cinema

Big Picture ❷ 3D

Looking for dinner and a movie all in one? Big Picture, a cozy Belltown eatery/theater, serves a full dinner menu (including a full bar) for each showing. *2505 1st Ave, 206/256-0566, thebigpicture.net*

Cinerama ❷ 3E

For some reason, popcorn just tastes better in front of a 90-foot-long screen. This, one of only three remaining theaters in the world capable of showing three-panel Cinerama films (others are in L.A. and London), was updated with state-of-the art sound and projection technologies in 1999. *2100 4th Ave, 206/441-3653, cinerama.com*

Harvard Exit ❶ 2C

The ivy-covered brick façade and ball-room-style lobby in this historic art house theater at the north end of Capitol Hill are alone worth the visit. The film menu is heavy on indie and foreign flicks. *807 E Roy St, 206/323-8986, landmarktheatres.com*

Majestic Bay ❶ 1B

Ballard's Bay Theater was bought in 1998 with the intention of refurbishing it. But the old wooden structure soon proved inadequate, and a new theater with a historic look was built on the site. The result became an instant classic. *2044 NW Market St, 206/781-2229, www.majesticbay.com*

Pacific Place Cinema ❷ 3F

Atop the six-story Pacific Place shopping mall, the 11-screen Pacific Place Cinema is downtown Seattle's most luxurious multiplex, favored by Downtown shoppers and movie mavens in search of perfect sound. *600 Pine St, #400, 206/652-2404, pacificplaceseattle.com*

Getting the 411

The best Seattle entertainment guides are online: Citysearch (seattle.citysearch .com), *Seattle Weekly* (seattle weekly.com), and the *Seattle Times* (nwsource.com); the latter two are also in print. Some of the best city blogs, with often witty cultural and political commentary, include Seattlest (seattlest.com) and Metroblogging Seattle (seattle.metblogs.com). But the most-read—and by far the most entertaining—blog in the city is *Slog* (slog.the stranger.com), operated by the editors of The Stranger. Slog has the best in upcoming live music, author readings, theater, and more.

Classical Music

Seattle Symphony ❷ 4F

Since 1985 conductor Gerard Schwarz has steered the Seattle Symphony to national prominence. Performances are at Downtown's Benaroya Hall, built in 1998 for a cool $120 million and renowned for its superb acoustics, plush seating, elegant lighting, and beautiful sightlines. *Benaroya Hall, 200 University St, 206/215-4800, seattle symphony.org*

Comedy

Comedy Underground ❷ 5B

Seattle's premier comedy club, in Pioneer Square, Comedy Underground hosts comics every night of the week, including a variety of local and national touring acts. *222 S Main St, 206/628-0303, comedyunderground .com*

Giggles ❶ 1C

This University District comedy outpost attracts national touring talent that includes top-notch veterans as well as up-and-comers. *Cash only.*

5220 Roosevelt Way NE, 206/526-5653, gigglescomedyclub.com

Jet City Improv ❶ 1C

Seattle's resident troupe of improv comedians performs every Friday and Saturday night at their University District theater; all shows are appropriate for the whole family. 5510 University Way NE, 206/781-3879, jetcityimprov.com

Dance

On the Boards ❶ 2B

Founded in 1978, On the Boards has made its reputation as a first-class theater by hosting cutting-edge performing artists. Notable performers have included the northwest troupe 33 Fainting Spells, Laurie Anderson, and Bill T. Jones. 100 W Roy St, 206/217-9886, ontheboards.org

Pacific Northwest Ballet ❷ 1D

With a company of 44 highly trained dancers, Pacific Northwest Ballet (PNB) has distinguished itself as one of North America's best ballet companies. The season runs September through June, with performances at the Seattle Center's Marion Oliver McCaw Hall. 301 Mercer St, 206/441-2424, pnb.org

---

New-Music City

Since the advent of grunge rock and the massive rise to fame of bands like Nirvana, Pearl Jam, and Soundgarden in the early 1990s, Seattle has rightfully been considered a pioneer of new music—especially lo-fi, countercultural, anti-pop music. The 21st century has seen a new wave of homegrown acts, led by indie-rock bands like Death Cab for Cutie and Modest Mouse, and Seattle's clubs and rock venues remain as vibrant as ever. The best spots for live shows are Neumo's and Chop Suey (Capitol Hill), the Showbox (Downtown), and the High Dive (Fremont).

UW World Series ❹

Held October through May at Meany Hall on the University of Washington campus, this series of dance and music performances by international artists has included the Sydney Dance Company, the Parsons Dance Company, and many others. University of Washington, Meany Hall, NE 40th St at 15th Ave NE, 206/543-4882, uwworldseries.org

Velocity Dance Theater ❷ 3H

A hotbed of local talent, Velocity mounts innovative modern dance performances in the unique setting of OddFellows Hall, a historic Capitol Hill landmark. 915 E Pine St, #200, 206/325-8773, velocitydancecenter.org

Jazz

Dimitriou's Jazz Alley ❷ 3E

In an alley near the intersection of 6th Avenue and Lenora Street, Dmitriou's is Seattle's premier supperclub, hosting jazz icons throughout the year. Past performers include McCoy Tyner, Oscar Peterson, and Ray Brown.

Closed Mon. 2033 6th Ave, #255, 206/441-9729, jazzalley.com

Triple Door ❷ 4F

When it comes to intimacy and luxury, few venues rival the Triple Door. Its Mainstage regularly hosts local and national jazz acts and has a stunning, sloped viewing area with semicircular booths and table service. *216 Union St, 206/838-4333, thetripledoor.net*

Jazz Seattle-style

Tula's ❷ 3E

Fans of gritty, close-quarters jazz clubs will feel right at home at Tula's, a Belltown jazz joint that has a devoted local following and music every night of the week. *2214 2nd Ave, 206/443-4221, tulas.com*

Rock & Pop

Chop Suey ❶ 3C

Rather than noodles this Capitol Hill club serves up a revolving menu of hip-hop, electronica, and rock. It's a place to see and be seen for a young, stylish crowd that thickens as the clock approaches midnight. *1325 E Madison St, 206/324-8000, chopsuey.com*

High Dive ❶ 1C

Fremont's most reliable live music venue features local rock acts nightly. The quarters can be a bit cramped, especially on the weekends, but the crowds don't mind getting friendly. *513 N 36th St, 206/632-0212, high diveseattle.com*

Standing room only

Little Red Hen (off map)

Home turf of Seattle's urban cowboys and cowgirls, the Little Red Hen, in Greenlake, 4 miles north of Fremont, offers up country music six nights a week and draws boot-scootin' crowds for dance lessons (Sun and Tues), karaoke (Wed), and live shows (Thurs–Sat). *7115 Woodlawn Ave NE, 206/522-1168, littleredhen.com*

Neumo's ❷ 3H

One of the city's larger clubs, Neumo's attracts national touring acts on a weekly basis. Bookings appeal mostly to fans of indie rock, hip-hop, and electronica. The Capitol Hill club hosts all-ages shows on select nights. *925 E Pike St, 206/709-9647, neumos.com*

Showbox ❷ 3B

Since opening in 1939 the Showbox has hosted countless rock, hip-hop, jazz, and pop shows by artists of local and national renown. Duke Ellington once took the stage here, as did Muddy Waters, the Ramones, and Pearl Jam. Today the expansive Downtown club is firmly entrenched as Seattle's signature rock venue. *1426 1st Ave, 206/628-3151, showboxonline.com*

Theater

A Contemporary Theatre (ACT) ❷ 3F

Since 1965 ACT has been producing contemporary classics by Tom Stoppard, Steve Martin, Neil Simon, and the like, as well as world premieres of new works by up-and-coming and established playwrights. *700 Union St, 206/292-7676, acttheatre.org*

Intiman Theatre ❷ 1D

Swedish for "the intimate," Intiman is just that: an intimate theater spotlighting contemporary works by local and national playwrights. On the Seattle Center campus, the Intiman's season runs from late March through December. *201 Mercer St, 206/269-1900, www.intiman.org*

Seattle Repertory Theatre ❷ 1D

Since its founding in 1963, Seattle Repertory has earned a reputation as a premier resident theater. Productions range from *Twelfth Night* to *The Breach*, a contemporary play about the devastations of Hurricane Katrina. *155 Mercer St, 206/443-2210, seattlerep.org*

Sports

Baseball

Seattle Mariners ❷ 7F

Safeco Field, a baseball venue that features a retractable roof, is the crown jewel of the Seattle sports stadiums. It's home to the Mariners, who, after several successful seasons in the last decade, have earned a devoted following. *1560 1st Ave S, 206/346-4001, mariners.mlb.com*

Basketball

Seattle SuperSonics ❷ 1C

The NBA's SuperSonics are the main draw at the Seattle Center KeyArena, which also hosts the occasional rock concert. KeyArena is also home to the WNBA's Seattle Storm (wnba.com/storm) and the Seattle Thunderbirds (seattlethunderbirds.com) of the Western Hockey League. *305 Harrison St, 206/684-7200, nba.com/sonics*

Baseball in the Emerald City

On sunny summer evenings there are few better spots in Seattle than a seat at Safeco Field, home of the Seattle Mariners, inaugurated in 1999. "The Safe" offers sweeping views of downtown Seattle, Elliott Bay, and the Olympic Mountains, making it one of the nation's most scenic ballparks. Its retractable roof, when open, overlaps the adjacent railroad tracks, and trains frequently sound their horns as they pass by during games. The Mariners, who play in the stadium from April through September, have had intermittent success in recent years, but their fans remain dedicated.

Biking, Jogging, & Blading

Burke-Gilman Trail ❹

Seattle's longest contiguous recreational trail, at 27 miles, runs from Ballard through the University District and beyond. The Burke is popular among cyclists, pedestrians, and inline skaters. Bicycle rentals are available at Montlake Bicycle Shop (❶ 2D *2223 24th Ave E, 206/329-7333, montlakebike.com*) and Recycled Cycles (❶ 1C *1007 NE Boat St, 206/547-4491, recycledcycles.com*). *seattle.gov/parks*

Canoeing & Kayaking

Northwest Outdoor Center ❶ 2C

This Lake Union institution has kayak rentals, instruction, and sales. Rent a kayak for an hour, a day, or more, and take the time to explore the region's stunning waterways. *2100 Westlake Ave N, 206/281-9694, nwoc.com*

Waterfront Activities Center ❶ 2D

On the shore of Union Bay, the Waterfront Activities Center (WAC) at the University of Washington rents aluminum canoes and rowboats. Adventurous canoeists often paddle through the winding channels of the adjacent Washington Park Arboretum. *3800 Montlake Blvd, 206/543-9433, depts.washington.edu/ima*

Football

Seattle Seahawks ❷ 6F

Seattle's beloved professional football team plays at Qwest Field. On game days throughout the fall, the area around Qwest is overrun by football fanatics dressed in all manner of Seahawks garb. *800 Occidental Ave S, 206/381-7940, seahawks.com*

University of Washington Huskies ❹

Husky Stadium sits on the shore of Union Bay, with the waters of Lake Washington and the Cascade Mountains visible from a majority of the seats. *3800 Montlake Blvd, 206/543-2200, gohuskies.cstv.com*

*Sailing boat on Lake Union
with Seattle skyline*

Golf

West Seattle Golf Course ● 4B

This surprisingly scenic West Seattle municipal golf course has copious views of Downtown from the back nine, and Mt. Rainier can be glimpsed from the first tee. Rentals and instruction are available. *4470 35th Ave SW, 206/935-5187, seattlegolf.com*

Sailing

Center for Wooden Boats ● 2C

Rent rowboats and sailboats at this maritime center at the south end of Lake Union. The staff is a friendly, knowledgeable crew of boatbuilders and sailing instructors. Rowboats may be rented by the half hour; sailboats require a minimum one-hour rental. *1010 Valley St, 206/382-2628, cwb.org*

seattle places to eat and drink

Seattle's booming and increasingly progressive population is fueling a renaissance of locally grown cuisine. At one time, seafood may have been the only local product on the menu, but today you'll find local cheeses, breads, wines, meats, and produce. The city also has an array of international cuisines: Asian Pacific food is thriving, as always, and beyond the borders of the International District; authentic taco trucks can be found in many industrial areas; and new Italian restaurants are practically reinventing the genre. Whatever your tastes, Seattle's restaurants don't disappoint.

taste it places to eat and drink

Asian

Shiro's $$$ ❷ 3E

Eat-and-run sushi spots can be found all over town, but Shiro's, in Belltown, has some of Seattle's freshest fish and most authentic sushi. Chef Shiro Kashiba buys only the best cuts of tuna, *unagi* (eel), salmon, and other fish. Highlights include the smelt tataki and the sashimi platter. *No lunch. 2401 2nd Ave, 206/443-9844, shiros.com*

Tamarind Tree $$ ❶ 3C

This semi-swanky café serves Vietnamese cuisine in a romantic, candlelit atmosphere that can't be found elsewhere in the International District. The crepe stuffed with scallops, prawns, pork, shiitake mushroom, bean sprouts, and mung beans is simply awesome. *1036 S Jackson St, Unit A, 206/860-1404, tamarindtreerestaurant.com*

Thai Tom $ ❶ 1C

The only drawback to this ultra-casual University District favorite is the tiny seating area. Our suggestions: Arrive early, don't bring a party of more than two, and don't miss the Swimming Rama—chicken in peanut sauce served over a bed of steamed spinach and rice. *4543 University Way NE, 206/548-9549*

Wild Ginger $$$ ❷ 2F

This is one of the city's highest-grossing restaurants, and for good reason. In the heart of Downtown, directly across Union Street from Benaroya Hall, Wild Ginger serves outstanding pan-Asian, Pacific Rim–influenced fare. The atmosphere is bustling, lively, and welcoming, but decidedly hip. *No lunch Sun. 1401 3rd Ave, 206/623-4450, wildginger.net*

Bistros

Café Campagne $$$ ❷ 4E

Fine French cuisine is served in a warm, slightly-bohemian dining room that could easily be mistaken for a Parisian bistro. Steps from the Pike Place Market, it's a favorite of critics and casual diners alike. Menu highlights include cassoulet of white bean stew with lamb, pork, duck confit, and garlic sausage, and the roasted half chicken with shallots, yellow potatoes, and *pan jus. Also serves brunch Sat–Sun. 86 Pine St, 206/728-2233, campagnerestaurant.com*

Dinette $$$ ❷ 2G

In a cozy Capitol Hill space, Dinette serves up reliably impressive rustic European fare. Chefs focus on in-season produce; a recent standout dish featured steamed mussels with green apple, cremini mushrooms, bacon, parsley, and Calvados cream. *No lunch; closed Sun–Mon. 1514 E Olive Way, 206/328-2282, dinetteseattle.com*

Le Pichet $$$ ❷ 2B

Just above the Pike Pace Market, this elegant, white-linened bistro serves up modern versions of French classics

---

Price Per Person
Prices based on three courses without alcohol.

$	Under $20
$$	$20–$30
$$$	$30–$50
$$$$	$50 and up

The Espresso Empire

Considered the birthplace of the American espresso boom, Seattle is where Starbucks, Seattle's Best Coffee, and Tully's Coffee were founded. (The first Starbucks store is still in operation in the Pike Place Market, at 1912 Pike Place.) Despite the massive commercial success of these brands, Seattle retains the independent spirit that gave rise to the art-house coffee scene, and today, independent cafés and roasters can be found in every neighborhood, and in some cases on nearly every corner. Space doesn't allow for a complete listing, but quintessential Seattle coffeehouses are Herkimer Coffee (*7320 Greenwood Ave N, 206/784-0202, herkimercoffee.com*), Espresso Vivace (❷ *2G 227 Yale Ave N, 206/388-5164*), and Fuel Coffee (❶ *2D 610 19th Ave E, 206/329-4700, fuelcoffeeseattle.com*).

such as *choucroute garnie* (sauerkraut simmered with smoked pork sausage, white sausage, ham hock, and caraway) and *poulet rôti* (chicken roasted to order in beef broth with turnips, potatoes, and escarole). *Also serves breakfast daily. 1933 1st Ave, 206/256-1499, lepichetseattle.com*

Restaurant Zoe $$$ ❷ 3E

A cozy, lamp-lit Belltown hideaway, Zoe serves a menu of simple, hearty dishes crafted from the freshest local ingredients. Favorite entrees include braised beef short rib with fingerling potatoes, fresh grated horseradish, pickled red onion, and watercress. *No lunch. 2136 2nd Ave, 206/256-2060, restaurantzoe.com*

Breakfast Champions

Café Presse $$ ❶ 3C

Pain au chocolat (bittersweet chocolate melted on a baguette) and *croque madam* (baked ham, Gruyère, béchamel, and egg sandwich) are standbys at this French café. Simpler, more casual, and more affordable than sister restaurant Le Pichet, Café Presse televises European soccer matches on weekends and has free Wi-Fi. *Also serves breakfast daily. 1117 12th Ave, 206/709-7674, cafepresse seattle.com*

St. Cloud's $$ ❶ 3D

In the leafy Madrona neighborhood, east of Capitol Hill, this family-friendly café is a community gathering spot. Breakfast favorites include the house-made corned-beef hash and the Imperial Mix Up—rice, scallions, eggs, ginger, and Portuguese sausage, all scrambled together. *Serves breakfast Sat–Sun; no lunch weekdays. 1131 34th Ave, 206/726-1522, stclouds.com*

Burgers & Beyond

King's Hardware $$ ❶ 1B

The latest in Seattle's expanding family of retro-pubs, King's has walls adorned with a staggering amount of taxidermy and on-site diversions such

Now that's a hearty burger

as Skee-Ball. The burger menu is top-notch; it includes the After School Special, topped with peanut butter and bacon. *No lunch weekdays. 5225 Ballard Ave NW, 206/782-0027*

Palace Kitchen $$$ ❷ 3E

The sublime food—which includes whole grilled trout and a chorizo-and-sheep-cheese omelet—can hardly be classified as pub grub, but Palace Kitchen nonetheless has one of the city's best burgers, made with wood-grilled Oregon country beef. And it's a rare opportunity to chase a burger with crème caramel. *No lunch. 2030 5th Ave, 206/448-2001, tom douglas.com*

Red Mill Burgers $ (off map)

Winner of the *Seattle Weekly's* best burger contest for 10 years running, Red Mill favorites include the verde burger, with fire-roasted Anaheim peppers, Jack cheese, and the famous Mill sauce (the recipe, unfortunately, is a secret). The casual, retro-styled burger joint/diner is on Phinney Ridge, 4 miles north of Fremont. *No credit cards. Closed Mon. 312 N 67th St, 206/783-6362, redmillburgers.com*

Smith $$$ ❶ 2D

The "gastropub" menu at this taxidermy-adorned hunting-lodge-style restaurant in Capitol Hill is full of modern comfort food, including "devils on horseback"—figs stuffed with blue cheese, then wrapped in bacon; deviled eggs; and a basic burger served with excellent sweet-potato fries. Smith also offers a solid selection of beers and spirits. *332 15th Ave E, 206/322-9420*

The Finest Dining

Canlis $$$$ ❶ 2C

Founded in 1950, Canlis has been entertaining celebrities, dignitaries, and Seattle foodies ever since, thanks to timeless classics such as Black Angus filet mignon and sesame-encrusted mahimahi with mango coulis. On the northeast slope of Queen Anne Hill, it has stunning views of Lake Union. *Closed Sun. No lunch. 2576 Aurora Ave N, 206/283-3313, canlis.com*

Le Gourmand $$$$ ❶ 1B

An inconspicuous little brick building on a busy corner in Ballard is an unlikely location for the most exquisite French cuisine in town. Order from the menu or opt for a multicourse tasting experience, which might include shrimp moussaline, halibut with puff pastries in a tarragon cream sauce, and crème brulee. *No lunch; closed Sun–Tues. 425 NW Market St, 206/784-3463*

Rover's $$$$ ❶ 2D

James Beard award–winning chef/owner Thierry Rautureau (aka

"The Chef in the Hat," for his ever-present fedora) has created an intimate yet casual atmosphere in which visitors can enjoy his unparalleled creations. Among the many highlights is Maine lobster with English cucumber, white sturgeon caviar, and champagne dressing. *No lunch Sat–Thurs; closed Sun. 2808 E Madison St, 206/325-7442, rovers-seattle.com*

Sitka & Spruce $$$ ❶ 2C

Chef Matt Dillon opened this hole-in-the-wall in Seattle's Eastlake neighborhood in 2006, quickly earning critical and popular acclaim. It's a good bet for adventurous food lovers—past dishes have included pickled fiddlehead ferns with halibut cheeks—who don't mind communal seating in the small dining room. *Also serves breakfast Sat–Sun; no lunch; closed Mon. 2238 Eastlake Ave E, 206/324-0662, sitkaandspruce.com*

Latin Flavor

El Puerco Lloron $ ❷ 2A

"The Crying Pig," serves up authentic Mexican fare, including pork tacos and handmade corn tamales. The endearing, cafeteria-style taqueria is in the Pike Street Hillclimb, a pedestrian park just downhill from the Pike Place Market. *No dinner Sun. 1501 Western Ave, #200, 206/624-0541*

Gordito's Healthy Mexican Food $ (off map)

Known for massive, football-size burritos (the large could feed four) with fillings from steak to prawns, this Phinney Ridge restaurant also has fajitas, enchiladas, tacos, and quesadillas. Ingredients are fresh, the salsa is excellent, and vegetarian options are plentiful. *213 N 85th St, 206/706-9532, gorditoshealthy mexicanfood.com*

La Carta de Oaxaca $$ ❶ 1B

Empanadas, posole, and mole *negro Oaxaqueno* (made with black chilies and chicken or pork) highlight this menu focusing exclusively on the Oaxaca region of southern Mexico. La Carta is in a beautiful space on historic Ballard Avenue; expect lines at peak lunch and dinner hours—reservations are not taken. *Closed Sun. No lunch Mon. 5431 Ballard Ave NW, 206/782-8722, lacartadeoaxaca.com*

Paseo Caribbean Restaurant $ ❶ 1C

This Fremont sandwich shop has become a lunchtime mecca. The Cuban-style roasted pork, chicken, and tofu sandwiches are absolute heaven. Lines form by 1pm, so arrive early. *No credit cards. Closed Sun–Mon. 4225 Fremont Ave N, 206/545-7440*

New Northwestern

Boat Street Café $$$ ❷ 2C

Formerly on Boat Street—hence the name—this upscale lower Queen Anne café serves fresh seafood, lamb, and pork, with a French flair. Alaskan king salmon, roasted rib-eye with nicoise olive tapenade, and hedgehog mushroom flan highlight the menu. *Also serves brunch daily; no dinner Sun–Mon. 3131 Western Ave, 206/632-4602, boatstreetcafe.com*

Crush $$$ ❶ 2D

The brainchild of chef Jason Wilson and his wife, Nicole, Crush is in a beautifully converted Tudor home in Capitol Hill. Local, organic ingredients are the building blocks for seasonal dishes such as chantarelle raviolo in Hubbard squash *jus*. There are few more romantic tables in town. *No lunch; closed Sun–Mon. 2319 E Madison St, 206/302-7874, chefjasonwilson.com*

Earth & Ocean $$$ ❷ 4F

Chef Adam Stevenson deals with local, organic produce, meats, and seafoods at this chic spot in the W Hotel downtown. The charcuterie—cured and smoked sausages, pickled vegetables, and sweet and savory jams—is made in-house. Celebrity sightings are relatively frequent at the adjoining W Bar. *Also serves breakfast daily. 1112 4th Ave, 206/264-6060, earthocean.net*

Tilth $$ ❶ 1C

Founded in 2005 by chef Maria Hines, highly acclaimed Tilth, in Wallingford, 2 miles northeast of Fremont, specializes in dishes featuring local organic ingredients, such as squash *carnaroli*-rice risotto to Skagit River Ranch pork belly. The restaurant is in a homelike

Wild Salmon: a Local Delicacy

Seattle sits at the nexus of the wild salmon industry. In addition to fish harvested from Washington's waters, the city's restaurants have excellent access to salmon caught in British Columbia and Alaska. Spring- and summer-run chinook (or king) is in the greatest demand, and for good reason: the fish is deliciously rich, thanks to its relatively high oil content. (Better still is the elusive ivory king, a rare sub-species with white flesh that's even richer than its brethren's.) Other salmon species include coho (or silver), another highly sought fish; keta (or chum); sockeye (or red); and pink (or humpback). All varieties can be found in the restaurants of the Pacific Northwest, so when ordering salmon, it's easy to go wild.

craftsman bungalow complete with porch rockers. *Closed Mon. Also serves brunch Sat–Sun.; no lunch weekdays. 1411 N 45th St, 206/633-0801, tilth restaurant.com*

Union $$$ ❷ 4F

The food and atmosphere are simple, elegant, and earthy at this downtown restaurant. In his first venture, chef Ethan Stowell incorporates the best of seasonal local and far-reaching ingredients in dishes like grilled octopus with marinated beets and blood orange. *No lunch. 1400 1st Ave, at Union St, 206/838-8000, unionseattle.com*

Pizza

Piecora's New York Pizza $ ❶ 2C

New York–style pizza rules the day at this Capitol Hill hangout, but the pastas, salads, and calzones are delicious as well. Piecora's has presided over this intersection since 1982—longer than most of its patrons have been alive. *1401 E Madison St, at 14th Ave E, 206/322-9411, piecoras.com*

Serious Pie $$$ ❷ 3E

Tom Douglas—Seattle's celebrity chef extraordinaire—has entered new territory with this downtown haute-pizza enclave, opened in 2006. Top sellers include a cherry-bomb-pepper and sweet fennel sausage pizza that never fails to impress. No lunch Sun. 316 Virginia St, 206/838-7388, tomdouglas .com

Tutta Bella $$ ❶ 1C

This spacious restaurant in Wallingford, 2 miles northeast of Fremont, serves Neapolitan-style pies—like the Antica, with Genoa salami, herb mushrooms, fresh mozzarella, roasted red peppers, and Grana Padano cheese—with skill and panache. Tutta Bella also brews its own lager and produces its own wine. 4411 Stone Way N, 206/633-3800, tuttabellapizza.com

Via Tribunali $ ❸ 3H

With exposed brick walls and gothic chandeliers, warm, dimly lit Via Tribunali, on Capitol Hill, feels almost medieval. The pies, baked in a wood-burning Vesuvius brick oven, and made with authentic ingredients like prosciutto crudo and mozzarella di bufala (buffalo-milk cheese), are truly Neapolitan. No lunch. 913 E Pike St, 206/322-9234, viatribunali.com

Seafood

Etta's $$$ ❷ 3E

Easy access to the freshest fish in town (just one block south at Pike Place Market), Etta's creates masterpieces like spice-rubbed, grilled wild salmon as well as a mean fish and chips. The place is elegant, dark, and romantic, and window-front tables offer sunset views of Elliott Bay. 2020 Western Ave, 206/443-6000, tomdouglas.com

The Oceanaire Seafood Room $$$$ ❷ 3F

Stepping inside this Downtown establishment is like boarding a ship: all smooth wood, polished brass, and plush booths, with suited power brokers frequently gathered at the bar for oysters and martinis. Everything, from shrimp scampi to lobster tail, is fresh and skillfully prepared. No lunch weekends. 1700 7th Ave, 206/267-2277, theoceanaire.com

Palisade Restaurant $$$ ❶ 2B

Across Elliott Bay from Downtown, Palisade presides over the Elliott Bay Marina at the base of Magnolia Bluff. The views of the downtown skyline are spectacular, as is the menu of fresh seafood, steaks, chops, and pupu platters such as the tower of teriyaki tenderloin, tiger prawns, and crab cakes. No lunch Sat. 2601 W Marina Pl, 206/285-1000, palisade restaurant.com

Waterfront Seafood Grill $$$ ❷ 3C

At the tip of Pier 70, the Waterfront has expansive views of Elliott Bay, the Space Needle, and Magnolia Bluff. It prides itself on its fresh seafood and top-tier wines; the menu includes king crab legs with champagne beurre blanc as well as steaks, chops, and roast duck and chicken. No lunch. 2801 Alaskan Way, Pier 70, 206/956-9171, waterfrontpier70.com

Tables with a View

The forests, mountains, and water surrounding Seattle make for some superb scenery, so it's only natural that a host of local restaurants would accompany dinner with views. Some of the best: Canlis has an amazing vista of Lake Union and the Cascade Mountains; the waterfront Palisade Restaurant looks south at downtown Seattle and Mount Rainier beyond; Salty's (❶ 3B *1936 Harbor Ave SW, 206/937-1600, saltys.com*) on Alki Beach, a West Seattle landmark, has an unbeatable view of Downtown; and Six Seven (❶ 3C *Edgewater Hotel, 2411 Alaskan Way, 206/269-4575, edgewaterhotel.com*) is a hip waterfront grill with a panorama of Elliott Bay and the Olympic Mountains beyond.

Steak, Seattle-Style

Daniel's Broiler $$$$ ❶ 2C

The only restaurant in Seattle that serves exclusively USDA Prime steaks, Daniel's flash-sears them, with optional toppings such as bleu cheese, peppercorn brandy sauce, or Dungeoness crab. Some surf joins the turf on the menu. Lake views, fine wines, and a piano bar add to the appeal. *No lunch weekends. 809 Fairview Pl N, 206/621-8262, www.schwartzbros.com*

El Gaucho $$$$ ❷ 3D

Steak lovers rave about El Gaucho's combination of premium beef, top-flight service, and lively atmosphere. Prepare to be pampered by a waitstaff that's among the best in the business at this Belltown establishment. *No lunch. 2505 1st Ave, 206/728-1337, elgaucho.com*

Jak's Grill $$$ ❶ 4B

This unpretentious steakhouse has quietly made a name for itself with some of the finest steaks and chops in the Northwest. The West Seattle location is bedecked with high-backed wooden booths, stellar cocktails, and a gregarious and professional staff. *No lunch Sun–Mon. 4548 California Ave SW, 206/937-7809, jaksgrill.com*

Metropolitan Grill $$$$ ❷ 5F

This luxury steakhouse in the heart of Downtown headlines mouthwatering steaks and chops, including USDA Prime New York peppercorn steak and blackened Prime Rib with a Cajun crust. The sommelier is one of the best in the business and the wine list is expertly crafted. *No lunch weekends. 820 2nd Ave, 206/624-3287, themetropolitangrill.com*

Bars
Polished

The Alibi Room ❷ 4E

This sultry alley hideway with exposed-brick walls is popular with hip downtown workers escaping the Pike Place Market mobs. *85 Pike St, #410, 206/623-3180, seattlealibi.com*

Black Bottle ❷ 3D

Candlelight, towering ceilings, and upscale pub fare appeal to the twenty-

and thirty-somethings who flock to this Belltown bar. *2600 1st Ave, 206/441-1500, blackbottleseattle.com*

Chapel ❷ 7G

In a former funeral home on Capitol Hill, soaring ceilings and semi-gothic architecture mix with sleek modern furnishings and stiff drinks. *1600 Melrose Ave, 206/447-4180, thechapelbar.com*

Purple Café & Wine Bar ❷ 4F

Chic industrial décor and an expansive wine list are the draws at this favorite après-work destination for Downtown suits. *1225 4th Ave, 206/829-2281, thepurplecafe.com*

Sambar ❶ 1B

Diminutive but upscale, this cozy Ballard cocktail bar next to Le Gourmand has eclectic concoctions such as the pungent "gingerini." *5416 6th Ave NW, 206/781-4883*

Tarnished

College Inn Pub ❶ 1C

Over a dozen beers are on tap at this semi-bohemian subterranean watering hole with secretive back-room booths. *4006 University Way NE, 206/634-2307, collegeinnseattle.com*

Hazlewood ❶ 1B

With tight quarters, standout cocktails, and a hip, young-ish crowd, this Ballard bar is an excellent spot to make new friends. *2311 NW Market St, 206/783-0478*

The Hideout ❷ 4G

Local art fills this Capitol Hill speakeasy that's equal parts gallery and bar; eclectic cocktails are made with fresh-squeezed juices. *1005 Boren Ave, 206/903-8480, hideoutseattle.com*

Linda's Tavern ❷ 3H

Capitol Hill's indie-rocker epicenter, dimly lit Linda's is packed nightly. The drinks are strong; the characters off the wall. *707 E Pine St, 206/325-1220*

White Horse Trading Company ❷ 4E

Regulars love this discreet little pub and bookstore for its "hidden" alley access, vintage furniture, friendly bartenders, and dogs-welcome policy. *1908 Post Alley, 206/441-7767*

Microbrew Metropolis

Seattle is a hotbed of craft breweries (microbreweries). Beer lovers in the Emerald City have a huge selection of local brews to choose from, ranging from the ultra-hoppy IPAs of Maritime Pacific Brewery (❷ 7F *1514 NW Leary Way, 206/782-6181, maritimebrewery.com*) to the malty browns of Elysian Brewing (❶ 2C *1221 E Pike St, 206/860-1920, elysianbrewing .com*). Visiting a local craft brewery is recommended; many brewers offer complimentary or low-priced tastings. Some of the best breweries to visit include Hale's Ales (❶ 1B *4301 Leary Way NW, 206/706-1544, halesales.com*) in Ballard; Red Hook (*14300 NE 145th St, Woodinville, 425/483-3232, red hook.com*), 15 miles northwest of Seattle, and Pyramid Brewery (❷ 7F *1201 1st Ave S, 206/682-3377, pyramidbrew.com*), south of Downtown.

seattle practical information

Seattle is flanked by bodies of water and mountain ranges to the east and west, which can lead to some mixups for newcomers. Furthermore, the city is bisected by the Lake Washington Ship Canal and crossed by five major bridges. Thanks to this geographical conundrum and a booming population, driving conditions range from fair to gridlocked. Many of Seattle's satellite neighborhoods—including Ballard, the University District, and Queen Anne—are miles apart, which makes for tough walking. Thankfully many top attractions are Downtown, or within a 10-minute walk of Downtown. If you're staying in the Downtown area, you won't need to bother with wheels, but if you're venturing farther afield, consider renting a car.

know it practical information

Tourist Info

Visitor Centers

Seattle Visitors Center & Concierge Services ❷ 3G

In the Washington State Convention and Trade Center, in downtown Seattle. *7th Ave and Pike St, 206/461-5840, visitseattle.org*

Arriving by Air

Seattle is served by one commercial airport: Seattle-Tacoma International.

Seattle-Tacoma International (SEA) ❶ 7C

"SeaTac" is the largest airport in the Pacific Northwest and the primary domestic and international hub for the Puget Sound region. The airport is 14 miles (about a 30-minute drive) south of downtown Seattle. Its central terminal, renovated in 2005, has many dining and shopping choices. *206/433-5388, portseattle.org/seatac*

To and from the Airport by Bus

Metro Transit has a variety of affordable bus routes that serve the airport, but they are quite a bit slower than private options such as the Downtown Airporter, a Gray Line bus service.

Metro Transit route 174

Travels between the airport and Downtown daily from 4:30 am until 2 am, departing twice per hour. The trip costs $1.75 each way (50¢ for children ages 6–17); travel time ranges from 40 minutes to an hour, depending on traffic. *206/553-3000, transit.metrokc.gov*

Gray Line Seattle Downtown Airporter

Shuttles between the airport and major Downtown hotels from 5 am until 11 pm daily; buses depart twice per hour. The trip takes from 35 to 60 minutes, depending on traffic, and costs $10.25 one-way or $17.00 round-trip ($7.25 and $10.00 for children ages 2–12.) *206/626-6088, graylineseattle .com*

To and from the Airport by Train

At this writing Sound Transit's Link Light Rail is scheduled to begin service from SeaTac to Downtown Seattle in late 2009. *206/398-5000 or 800/201-4900, soundtransit.org*

To and from the Airport by Taxi

Taxis are a primary mode of transport to and from SeaTac. The time savings are clear—taxis typically travel from Downtown to the airport in 20 to 25 minutes, depending on traffic, and they're available around the clock. Fares average between $30 and $35. *Orange Cab: 206/522-8800, orange cab.net. Yellow Taxi: 206/622-6500, yellowtaxi.net*

Getting Around

Seattle isn't particularly dense, so getting from one neighborhood to another involves some travel. (However, plenty of Seattle's neighborhoods offer a full day's worth of pedestrian-friendly entertainment and window shopping—especially Ballard, Fremont, and Capitol Hill). Driving is the easiest option, though traffic can be hairy during rush hour. For those without a car, the most popular alternative is the bus system, which may strike you as overcrowded, difficult to navigate, and painfully slow. Taxis are a convenient option, albeit expensive. Bicycling is a great choice for those not averse to riding in the city—and in the rain.

Getting Around by Bicycle

Seattle has made many efforts to become a more bicycle-friendly city in the 21st century, and is home to more miles of bike lanes and paths than ever before. As a result, record numbers of Seattleites are choosing to commute by bicycle. Rentals are offered by several bike shops around the city, including those listed here.

Bikestation Seattle ❷ 6G
311 3rd Ave S, 206/332-9795, bikestation.org

Montlake Bicycle Shop ❶ 2D
2223 24th Ave E, 206/329-7333

Recycled Cycles ❶ 1C
1007 NE Boat St, 206/547-4491, recycledcycles.com

Getting Around by Bus

Metro Transit

The only bus-travel option in Seattle, Metro Transit's sytem is effective, if sometimes overcrowded. (Seattleites love to gripe about the city's lack of a rail-based public transit system, which forces most nondrivers to ride the bus.) Thankfully buses serve virtually every part of the city. Most buses run between 5 am and 1 am, although some routes operate 24 hours. Rush-hour trips (7 am–9 am and 4 pm–6 pm) are almost guaranteed to be standing-room only. Metro's online trip planner is a simple way to determine which route is best for you. Fares are $1.50 during nonpeak hours and $1.75 during peak hours (6 am–9 am and 3 pm–6 pm weekdays). *206/553-3000, transit.metrokc.gov*

Getting Around by Car

Despite serious congestion, driving remains the most convenient way to get around the city. (If it weren't, we wouldn't all be sitting in traffic, right?) While middays, evenings, and weekends are relatively devoid of serious backups, drivers can expect to find gridlock throughout the city during the morning and evening rush hours. If you must drive, avoid peak hours, especially on I-5, I-90, and SR-520.

Getting Around by Monorail or Streetcar

Seattle has no subway system, but it does have two small-scale rail systems. The most prominent—at a total distance of only 1 mile—is the monorail, which connects Downtown's Westlake Center with Seattle Center. The South Lake Union Streetcar, which opened in late 2007, runs between Downtown and South Lake Union, which offers access to the Center for Wooden Boats and a host of lakefront restaurants. At this writing the city is in early discussions to expand the minimally useful streetcar network.

Seattle Monorail

The monorail operates daily from 9 am until 11 pm. Trains run every 10 minutes from Westlake Center to Seattle Center. Roundtrip fares are $4.00 for adults, $1.50 for kids ages 5–12, and $2.00 for seniors over 65. *206/905-2600, seattlemonorail.com*

Seattle streetcar

Monorail traveling through EMP building

South Lake Union Streetcar

The Streetcar operates Mon through Thurs from 6 am until 9 pm, Fri and Sat from 6 am until 11 pm, and Sun from 10 am until 7 pm. Adult fares are $1.50; youth (ages 6–17) and senior (over 65) fares are 50¢. *206/553-3000, seattlestreetcar.org*

Getting Around by Taxi

Taxis are quite practical for shorter (less-expensive) trips—most residents use them for distances between 2 and 5 miles. Yellow Taxi is the most ubiquitous. Taxis can be hailed from most Downtown streets; in outlying neighborhoods, it's best to call.

Orange Cab
206/522-8800, orangecab.net
Yellow Taxi
206/622-6500, yellowtaxi.net

Banks

Most Seattle banks are open from 9 am until 6 pm weekdays, and 9 am until 1 pm on Sat. ATMs are found throughout the city, but they are most common Downtown. Most charge a service fee of at least $1.50 for non-customers; however, Seattle is rife with credit union ATMs, most of which do not levy a fee.

Changing Money

Seattle's currency is the US dollar, which comes in denominations of $1, $5, $10, $20, $50, and $100.

Coinage is denominated by 1¢, 5¢, 10¢, and 25¢. There are two Custom House Currency Exchange Centers in Seattle—one is at Pier 69, and the other at 911 Western Avenue. Most banks can exchange currencies but generally need advance notice to perform all but the most common currency exchanges, which means that currency exchange houses are usually the easier option.

Climate

Seattle's climate has an undeservedly bad rep. It enjoys a comfortable, temperate maritime climate year-round. On average Seattle receives less annual precipitation than New York and Washington, D.C. (Overcast skies are another matter). Winter temperatures average in the low 40s, and summertime temperatures average in the mid 70s, with nothing approaching East Coast summertime humidity.

Consulates

Australia ❶ 7E
401 Andover Park E, 206/575-7446

Canada ❷ 3F
413 Plaza 200 Building, 6th Ave and Stewart St, 206/728-5145

United Kingdom ❸ 5F
900 4th Ave, Suite 3001, 206/622-9255

Disabled Access

Seattle is an accessible city for those with disabilities. The city's Department of Planning and Development fully enforces the Americans with Disabilities Act Accessibility Guidelines, ensuring that all businesses and public spaces are accessible to everyone.

The Alliance for People with disAbilities

Supports equal access for residents with disabilities, and provides information and referral, peer support, and self-advocacy. *4649 Sunnyside Ave N, Suite 100, 206/545-7055, disability pride.org*

Emergencies

Dial 911 in any type of emergency.

Harborview Medical Center ❷ 5H
325 9th Ave, 206/744-3000, uwmedicine.org/facilities/harborview

Swedish Medical Center ❷ 4H
747 Broadway, 206/386-6000, swedish.org

University of Washington Medical Center ❹
1959 NE Pacific St, 206/598-3300, uwmedicine.org/facilities/uwmedical center

Internet Access

Wi-Fi and high-speed Internet is prevalent throughout the city at coffee shops, Internet cafés, and at larger hotels.

Cafés

The following have connected PCs for use.

Aurafice Internet & Coffee Bar ❷ 3H
616 E Pine St, 206/860-9977

Capitol Hill Internet Lounge & Eatery ❶ 2C
216 Broadway E, 206/860-6858

Online Coffee Co. ❷ 2H
*1111 1st Ave, 206/381-1911,
onlinecoffeeco.com*

Free Access

Seattle Public Library (all branches)
*Central branch, ❷ 4F 1000 4th Ave,
386-4636, spl.org*

Wi-Fi

Wireless has yet to be offered to the masses free of charge, but entrepreneurial folks have little difficulty tracking down a signal at numerous coffee houses, bars, and other businesses, although most of these locations require a minimum purchase of food or drink. (The public libraries, listed above, offer free Wi-Fi as well.)

Lost & Found

Seattle Tacoma International Airport

SeaTac requests that passengers report lost items via an online Lost Property Report, which can be found and submitted at *hosting.portseattle.org/lnfweb/default.aspx.* To arrange pickup of lost items, call *206/433-5312.*

Greyhound Bus Terminal:
206/628-5561

King Street Station (Amtrak service): *206/382-4125*

Opening Hours

Restaurants and Bars

All restaurants listed open daily for lunch and dinner, unless noted otherwise. Most restaurants serve dinner from 5 till 10, but several kitchens work until 11 or midnight on weekends. Bars are legally obligated to cease serving alcohol by 2 am.

Stores

All stores listed open daily unless noted otherwise.

Post Offices

The U.S. Postal Service has branches throughout the city. Hours vary, but all are open by 9 and close at 6 Mon through Fri. Some locations close on Saturday; those that are open close at 3. All offices are closed on Sun.

USPS Main Post Office ❷ 4F
301 Union St, 800/ASK-USPS, usps.com

Public Holidays

Jan 1	New Year's Day
3rd Mon Jan	Martin Luther King, Jr. Day
3rd Mon Feb	Presidents' Day
Last Mon May	Memorial Day
July 4	Independence Day
1st Mon Sept	Labor Day
4th Thurs Nov	Thanksgiving Day
Dec 25	Christmas

Telephones

All of urban Seattle lies within the 206 area code. It's not necessary to dial the area code when making a local call. For long-distance calls, dial a 1 +

area code + 7-digit number. For international calls, dial 011 + country code + phone number. Prepaid phone cards for long-distance or international calling can be found at convenience stores throughout the city.

Tipping

Seattleites usually tip at least 15% when dining out. If service is excellent, 20% is increasingly the norm. Taxi drivers expect the same rate. Most bartenders expect $1 to $2 per drink ordered at the bar, while baristas are generally happy to see their tip jar swell by $1 per espresso drink. At hotels, tipping around $2 is common for services provided by bell-

hops, doormen, and maids (per day); concierges may merit $3–$10, depending on the service.

Tours

Argosy Cruises

Seattle's preeminent marine touring company offers four cruises daily, covering such watery locales as Lake Washington, Lake Union, the Ballard Locks, and Elliott Bay. A can't-miss. *206/623-1445, argosycruises.com*

Gray Line of Seattle

Gray Line boasts a wide range of bus tours, including the ever-popular City Sights, a 3.5-hour jaunt that visits Fremont, Pioneer Square, the Interna-

tional District, and much more. *206/624-5077, graylineseattle.com*

Market Heritage Tour

Looking for oddball anecdotes and useful shopping tips when visiting the historic Pike Place Market? Look no further than this informative, entertaining tour of Seattle's signature attraction. *206/682-7453, pikeplace market.org*

Ride the Ducks

Grab a seat in a World War II–era amphibious vehicle and embark on a rollicking tour of Seattle's streets and waterways. A can't-miss for kids, jokesters, and free spirits. *206/441-3825, ridetheducksofseattle.com*

Seattle skyline

directory

From hotel listings to annual events to a quick guide to the local lingo, this directory has what you need to hit the ground running.

Key to Icons

- Room Service
- Restaurant
- Fully Licensed Bar
- En suite Bathroom
- @ Business Centre
- Health Centre
- Air Conditioning
- P Parking

Prices for Double Rooms

$$$$	More than $500
$$$	Between $300 and $500
$$	Between $150 and $299
$	Between $75 and $149

Places to stay

Seattle is a large-scale business and leisure-travel destination—the city hosted over 4.3 million hotel visitors in 2005—with a cornucopia of hotel options. With few exceptions, the closer a hotel is to the Downtown core, the more expensive it will be. Outlying neighborhoods have some less expensive motels, inns, and bed-and-breakfasts.

Posh

Fairmont Olympic Hotel $$$ ❷ 4F

Downtown's most prestigious address, the Fairmont Olympic attracts discerning guests. The hotel opened in 1924; its Italian Renaissance architecture projects glamour, elegance, and extravagance like no other building in town. Distinguished by impeccable service, stunning grounds, and an ideal location in the heart of Downtown, the Fairmont is poised to remain a signature destination for years to come. *411 University St, 206/840-8402, fairmont.com*

Hotel 1000 $$$ ❷ 5F

At First Avenue and Madison Street, Hotel 1000 has one of the most prestigious addresses in Seattle's hotel industry. Its modern glass and concrete tower is a symbol of the city's continued affluence, and the interior design is marked by polished steel, glimmering glass, and sleek contemporary furnishings. Rooms are luxurious yet subdued, and make for idyllic retreats. On-site restaurant Boka is making a name for itself, and service throughout the property draws rave reviews. *1000 1st Ave, 206/957-1000, hotel1000seattle.com*

Mayflower Park Hotel $$$ ❷ 3F

A grand tribute to the fine hotels of yesteryear, the Mayflower was built in 1927 and retains the period charm and elegance that distinguished it 80 years ago. The lobby has soaring ceilings, Victorian furnishings, and elaborate flower arrangements, while Oliver's airy cocktail lounge pours wicked martinis. Rooms are updated; though a bit on the smallish side by today's standards. The modern Andaluca Restaurant has curvaceous wooden booths and a Mediterranean-inspired menu. *405 Olive Way, 206/382-6990, mayflowerpark.com*

Sorrento Hotel $$$ ❷ 4G

Seattle's oldest continuously operating boutique hotel was built in 1908: Its first registered guest was President William Howard Taft. The ever-luxurious Sorrento sits atop First Hill, just east of Downtown; the building's old-world feel is apparent in its gated courtyard, abundant fireplaces, crystal chandeliers, and ornate woodwork. The Hunt Club and the Fireside Room—the on-site restaurant and bar, respectively—are dens of luxury, with plush leather furnishings, indoor palms, and gleaming silver. *900 Madison St, 206/622-6400, hotelsorrento .com*

Bed-and-Breakfast

The Bacon Mansion $$ ❶ 2C

This gorgeous, 9,000-square-foot English Tudor home has 11 spacious guest rooms. The property also has a manicured patio and a series of elegant day rooms with stained-glass windows, marble fireplaces, and a grand piano. The mansion, built in 1909 by Cecil Bacon, sits on the northwestern edge of Capitol Hill, within 4 miles of Downtown, Queen Anne, and the University District. Guests have complimentary Wi-Fi. *959 Broadway E, 206/329-1864, baconmansion.com*

11th Avenue Inn $ ❶ 2C

In the heart of Capitol Hill, the historic 11th Avenue Inn is in a classic 1906 Seattle home. Public rooms—a dining room, living room, and den—are decorated with antique furnishings, woven rugs, and polished brass lamps and sconces. Guest rooms are loaded with plush down comforters and beautiful hardwood floors. The Inn, which has free Wi-Fi and parking, is less than a five-minute walk from Capitol Hill's bustling shopping and dining district. *121 11th Ave E, 800/720-7161, 11thavenueinn.com*

Inn of Twin Gables $ ❶ 1B

In a beautiful Craftsman-style home on the quiet, residential west slope of Queen Anne Hill, this quaint inn has just three guest rooms, all with antique furnishings. A gourmet breakfast, which may include stuffed French toast, savory crepes, or a chile relleno frittata, is served each morning. There's little within walking distance, making this a better choice for those with rental cars or an affinity for the bus system. *3258 14th Ave W, 206/284-3979, innoftwingables.com*

Pensione Nichols $ ❷ 2B

One block from the Pike Place Market, Pensione Nichols has some of Seattle's best views of Elliot Bay and the Olympic Mountains. The Pensione has two suites with private baths and kitchens in addition to 10 rooms with four shared bathrooms. The quaint lobby has an excellent meet-up spot—yes, it has views, too, and leather sofas. Breakfasts are truly continental—just fruit, bread, jam, butter, coffee, and tea. *1923 1st Ave, #300, 206/441-7125, pensionenichols.com*

Boutique

The Alexis Hotel $$ ❷ 5F

In a building that has stood at the corner of First and Madison since 1901, the Alexis is a Seattle classic that, after a $10 million renovation in 2007, has never looked better. Each room is different, though all have down duvets, and may have exposed brick walls, leather furniture, and crown molding. A hallway serves as a rotating "gallery" of artwork by prominent local artists. The luxurious spa offers facials, body polishing, massages, and more. *1007 1st Ave, 206/382-6990, alexishotel.com*

Hotel Andra $$ ❷ 3E

Strikingly beautiful Hotel Andra pampers its guests as few other properties can. The interior design integrates light blues, tangerines, and beiges in a modern setting. A wood-burning fireplace greets guests in the hotel's living room, which resembles a futuristic hunting lodge of sorts. The lobby provides direct access to Lola, a smashingly hip Greek bistro next door. Rooms are equipped with goose-down comforters and pillows, spa robes, Frette towels, and Egyptian cotton linens. *2000 4th Ave, 206/448-8600, hotelandra.com*

Hotel Vintage Park $$ ❷ 4F

This lovely boutique is dedicated to celebrating Washington's increasingly popular wine country. It hosts nightly wine tastings, and each room is dedicated to a Washington State winery. Framed wine labels adorn the walls, and each room is equipped with literature about its sponsoring winery, along with a complimentary yoga program on the in-room TV. In addition to the wine, guests appreciate the complimentary Wi-Fi and valet parking. *1100 5th Ave, 206/624-8000, hotelvintagepark.com*

Inn at El Gaucho $$ ❷ 3D
🚿 🍴 🍸 🏠 ♨ ❄ 🅿

With just 18 suites, the Inn at El Gaucho is far from the large, impersonal hotels so common in the Downtown area. Sporting a "retro-swank" 1950s decor, it sits directly above El Gaucho, a Belltown steakhouse of much repute. Rooms have 32-inch plasma-screen TVs; Bose Wave stereos; down comforters, pillow-top queen beds with Anichini linens; and Riedel wine glasses. *2505 1st Ave, 206/728-1133, inn.elgaucho.com*

Business

Paramount Hotel $$ ❷ 3F
🚿 🍸 🏠 @ ♨ ❄ 🅿

On the eastern edge of Downtown just two blocks from the Washington State Convention and Trade Center, the Paramount is an ideal choice for convention attendees. The décor here is simple, but elegant: The lobby is adorned by a large, marble-framed fireplace, expansive floral-printed sofas, and mahogany tables. In addition to the on-site business center, the hotel's 146 guest rooms have dual phone lines, dedicated data ports, and wireless Internet. *724 Pine St., 206/292-9500, paramounthotelsseattle.com*

Sheraton Seattle $$ ❷ 3F
🚿 🍸 🏠 ♨ ❄ 🅿

In the heart of the Downtown business and financial district, this 1,258-room high-rise hotel has 47 meeting rooms and 75,000 square feet of meeting space. The atmosphere, defined by expansive lobby lounges bedecked with potted palms, plush armchairs, and gleaming glass tabletops, is decidedly corporate yet undeniably inviting. In short, it's a business traveler's dream. *1400 6th Ave, 206/621-9000, starwoodhotels.com*

W Seattle $$$ ❷ 4F
🚿 🍸 🏠 ♨ ❄ 🅿

The Seattle outpost of this über-sleek chain doesn't disappoint. Catering to chic, urbane business and leisure travelers, the hotel has a contemporary interior design, and rooms are highlighted by pillow-top beds with goose-down covers. It's a sweet retreat from the chaos of the city. *1112 4th Ave, 206/264-6000, starwoodhotels.com*

Watertown $$ ❶ 1C
🍸 🏠 ♨ ❄ 🅿

The University District's finest hotel has a wide array of complimentary amenities: a local shuttle, loaner bicycles, a daily breakfast bar, a nightly wine reception, and underground parking. Rooms come with robes, premium bedding, Aveda bath products, and high-speed Internet access. Watertown's decor is business-chic; floor-to-ceiling windows provide the lobby with ample daylight, and a clean, modern aesthetic rules the day in both the rooms and the lobby. *4242 Roosevelt Way NE., 206/826-4242, watertownseattle.com*

Budget

Ace Hotel $ ② 3D
🍴 ⛲

All rooms and public spaces at this Belltown hotel are original, eclectic, and modern, and staying at the Ace is a unique, indie-flavored experience. The rooms, some of which feature hardwood floors, are sleekly decorated and are painted in pure white, adding to the hotel's European-modern feel. Wi-Fi and a continental breakfast are included free of charge. Some rooms share bathrooms. *2423 1st Ave, 206/448-4721, theacehotel.com*

The Moore Hotel $ ② 3E
⛲

One of Downtown's few true budget hotels, the Moore has stood on the corner of 2nd Avenue and Virginia Street, just two blocks from the Pike Place Market, since 1907. Rooms are basic, to say the least. They have beds, simple furnishings, and a dated decor. The lobby space meets that description, too, but the price can't be beat. Some rooms have shared baths. *1926 2nd Ave, 206/448-4852, moorehotel.com*

Silver Cloud Inn $$ ① 2F
🛏 🍴 ⛲ @ 🏋 ❄ Ⓟ

Although it's a bit spendier than the average budget hotel, the University Silver Cloud Inn is a bargain relative to its many comforts. Rooms have free Wi-Fi and premium cable, breakfast is complimentary, and there's a Tuesday evening wine reception, a fitness center, and a business center. The hotel, which features a somewhat standard mid-priced modern decor in its lobby and rooms, is just two blocks north of University Village. *4725 25th Ave NE, 206/525-4612, silvercloud.com*

Sixth Avenue Inn $ ② 3F
🛏 🍴 ⛲ 🏋 ❄ Ⓟ

This casual, down-to-earth inn is just north of Downtown, within walking distance of Seattle Center. It's anything but flashy, but for those who place a premium on functionality and comfort, it's a great choice. All rooms have voicemail, coffee maker, hairdryer, bathrobes, and air conditioning. *2000 6th Ave, 206/441-8300, sixthavenueinn.com*

More Sights

Kerry Park ① 2C

Perched halfway up the south flank of Queen Anne Hill, this tiny park provides an iconic view of downtown Seattle, Elliott Bay, and, on clear days, Mount Rainier. It's an ideal destination for photographers, romantics, and stargazers. Sunsets are particularly enjoyable here; there's nothing like the sight of a glowing ferry plying the waters of Puget Sound while the Downtown lights begin to twinkle. For a breathtaking vista of the Olympic Mountains, continue a quarter-mile west along West Highland Drive. *Free. 211 W Highland Dr, 206/684-4075, seattle.gov/parks*

Madrona Park ① 3D

There are few better places for a summertime swim than the beach at this enclave on the west shore of Lake Washington; on clear days you have copious views of Lake Washington,

Mount Rainier, and the Cascade Mountains. The leafy park takes its name from a stand of Madrona trees that sits on the lakeshore. The former residence of the late, legendary Kurt Cobain is just across Lake Washington Boulevard. *Free. 853 Lake Washington Blvd, 206/684-4075, seattle.gov/parks*

Kids' Seattle

Essential sights for families with kids include the Burke Museum (see p 4), the Pacific Science Center (see p 9), the Aquarium (see p 10), and the Woodland Park Zoo (see p 14). The Experience Music Project (see p 5) is fun for older kids, and the **Seattle Children's Museum** (❷ 1D *305 Harrison St, 206/441-1768, thechildrensmuseum.org*) is a great stop for younger ones.

Annual Events

Northwest Folklife Festival (late May): The city's annual celebration of all things folk—including music, dance, art, crafts, and food—is held at Seattle Center on Memorial Day Weekend, in late May. Bonus: It's free. *206/684-7300, nwfolklife.org*

Seafair (early Jul–early Aug): A month-long tribute to the glory of summer. Featured events include the Torchlight Parade through Downtown and a culminating air show featuring the U.S. Navy's Blue Angels. *206/728-0123, seafair.com*

Bumbershoot (early Sept): Bumbershoot is the city's largest music festival—three days of rock, blues, jazz, and nearly everything else during Labor Day Weekend. *206/281-7788, bumbershoot.org*

Seattle International Film Festival (May–June): SIFF, a 25-day celebration of all types of cinema, begins in mid-May. And with 270 feature films and 140 shorts, the action doesn't stop until the last curtain closes. *siff.net*

Earshot Jazz Festival (Oct–Nov): This month-long jazz fest, which is celebrating its 20th anniversary in 2008, runs from mid-October to mid-November each year. It features over 70 performances by big names, new faces, and local standbys. *earshot.org/festival*

Further Reading

Newspapers

Seattle Post-Intelligencer
seattlepi.com

Seattle Times
seattletimes.com

Listings

NwSource.com
The most comprehensive online resource for entertainment, dining, shopping, and adventure.

Seattle Weekly
A reliable source for music, dining, and film recommendations. Free and available on newsstands and in businesses throughout the city.

The Stranger
The ironic tone and humorous content of *The Stranger* resonates with younger Seattleites. Its music and events calendar may be the best in town. Free every Wednesday; available on newsstands and in businesses throughout the city.

speak it

Separated by water, hills, and differing cultural attitudes, Seattle's many neighborhoods can cause confusion for the first-time visitor. Add in the fact that many residents have adopted pet names for each area, and you've got a full-on headache waiting to happen. Below, we've pieced together a brief guide to help you navigate the increasingly complex terrain of Seattle's slang neighborhood names. Use it wisely.

The Center of the Universe - Also known as Fremont. Few bother to argue with the title, which the neighborhood's famously eclectic residents have claimed since sometime in the early 1980s.

SoDo: The area south of Downtown, of course. Home to the city's sports stadiums, artists' lofts, and warehouse parties.

Freelard: This term of endearment applies to the industrial and residential area between Fremont and Ballard.

The Ave: For the record, the Ave—pronounced "avv"—is University Way NE, in the University District.

SLUT: A citizen-appropriated name for Seattle's unpopular South Lake Union Streetcar, which residents have taken to calling the South Lake Union Trolley—or SLUT, for short.

Pill Hill: This neighborhood, which lies atop a hill directly east of Downtown, is home to many of the city's hospitals and medical clinics. Hence the nickname.

The Freeway: This term is applied almost exclusively to Interstate 5, which runs through Downtown on a north-south axis.

The ID & the CD: Nope, we're not talking about licenses and albums. These two acronyms stand for the International District and the Central District, respectively.

The Mercer Mess: The area around Mercer Street, located at the south end of Lake Union, is known for its horrible traffic jams.

Snoose Junction: A late-1800s term for Ballard, which once was the last chance for outbound fishermen to buy their tobacco (or snoose, as it was called back then).

Tangletown: An affectionate name for the neighborhood north of N 50th Street and southeast of Greenlake, which is known for its twisting, tangled street grid.

index

A
Airport 50
Alki Beach Park 4
Annual events 61
Asian cuisine 40
B
Ballard 11
Banks 52–53
Barneys New York 23
Bars 46–47, 54
Baseball 34
Basketball 34
Biking 35, 51
Bistros 40–41
Blading 35
Boeing Future of Flight Aviation Center & Boeing Tour 4
Books & music 21–22
Boutiques 23
Breakfast spots 41
Broadway Market 25–26
Burgers & beyond 41–42
Burke Museum of Natural History and Culture 4–5
Buses 50
C
Canoeing 35
Capitol Hill 9
Cinema 30–31
Classical music 32
Climate 53
Clothes & accessories 22–23, 27
Coffee scene 41
Comedy 31–32
Consulates 53
D
Dance 32
Department stores 23–24
Design, furniture & 24–25
Disabled access 53

Discovery Park 5
Downtown 7
E
Emergencies 53
Entertainment guides 31
Espresso 41
Experience Music Project 5–6
F
Fine dining 42–43
Food & wine 24
Football 35
Fremont 11
Frye Art Museum 6
Furniture & design 24–25
Further reading 61
G
Gas Works Park 6–8
Gifts & souvenirs 25
Golf 36
Ground transportation 50
H
Henry Art Gallery 8
Hiram M. Chittenden Locks 8
Holidays 54
Hotels 56–60
I
Inline skating 35
Internet access 53–54
J
Jazz 32–33
Jogging 35
K
Kayaking 35
Kerry Park 60
Kids' Seattle 61
L
Latin cuisine 43
Listings 61
Lost and found 54
M
Macy's 23–24
Madrona Park 60–61
Malls 25–26

Markets 26–27
Microbreweries 47
Money (changing) 52–53
Monorail 51–52
Myrtle Edwards Park 8–9

N
New Northwestern cuisine 43–44
New-music sites 32
Newspapers 61
Nordstrom 24

O
Olympic Sculpture Park 9
Opening hours 54
Outdoor gear 26

P
Pacific Place 26
Pacific Science Center 9
Performing arts centers 30
Pike Place Market 9–10, 26
Pizza 44–45
Post offices 54
Public holidays 54
Public transportation 50–52
Puget Sound 17

Q
Queen Anne 13

R
Resources, other 61
Restaurants 38–47, 54
Rock & pop music 33–34

S
Sailing 36
Science Fiction Museum and Hall of Fame 5–6
Seafood 44, 45
Seattle Aquarium 10
Seattle Art Museum 10
Seattle Asian Art Museum and Volunteer Park 10–11
Shopping 18–27
Shopping areas 20–21
Sights 4–17

Space Needle 11–12
Speak it 62
Sporting goods 26, 27
Sports 34–36
Steak 46
Streetcar 51–52

T
Taxis 50, 52
Telephones 54–55
Theater 34
Tickets 30
Tipping 55
Tourist information 50
Tours 55
Trains 50. See also Monorail
Transportation 50–52

U
University District 15
University District Farmer's Market 26–27
University Village 26

V
Vintage clothes 27
Visitor centers 50

W
Washington Park Arboretum 12–13
Washington State Ferries at Pier 52 13
Waterfront 7
Wing Luke Asian Art Museum 14
Woodland Park Zoo 14–15

Seattle CityGuide
Writer: Nick Horton
Editor: Shannon Kelly

Cover design: Georgiana Goodwin
Original Popout maps design: CM Cartographics

Important Advice
Always call ahead to make sure shops and restaurants will be open when you show up. We've worked hard to make the text and maps accurate, but cities change fast, and it's better to be safe than sorry.

Text copyright © 2009 Morris Book Publishing, LLC
PopOut map copyright © 2009 Compass Maps, Ltd.

All rights reserved. No part of this book may be reproduced or transmitted in any form by any means, electronic or mechanical, including photocopying and recording, or by any information storage and retrieval system, except as may be expressly permitted by the publisher. Requests for permissions should be addressed to The Globe Pequot Press, Attn: Rights and Permissions Department, P.O. Box 480, Guilford, CT 06437

This PopOut map product, its associated machinery and format use, whether singular or integrated within other products, is subject to worldwide patents granted and pending, including EP1417665, CN ZL02819864.6, and CN ZL200620 006638.7. All rights reserved including design, copyright, trademark, and associated intellectual property rights. PopOut is a registered trademark and is produced under license by Compass Maps Ltd.

Photo Credits
Page 33l © 2008 Jupiterimages Corporation. From Shutterstock: 1t, 11r, 49, 50, 52l © Natalia Bratslavsky; 1m, 38 © michael ledray; 1b © Mark B. Bauschke; 3 © Nick Carver Photography; 4 © kwest; 5l © Kanwarjit Singh Boparai; 5r © Travis Hilliard; 6 © Harry Hu; 7t © Aaron Wood; 8 © Carlos Arguelles; 9 © Mark B. Bauschke; 10l © Poul Costinsky; 10r © Chris Bence; 11l © Glenn R. McGloughlin; 12l © Cliff Deputy; 12r, 56 © Hiep Nguyen; 13 © Stephen Strathdee; 14l © steve estvanik; 14r © Jessica Bopp; 15l © Joseph Becker; 15r, 26, 29, 30 © Barry Salmons; 16 © Mark R; 19 © Chad McDermott; 20 © Harry Hu; 21 TK © charles taylor; 22 © clarissa harwell; 24 © salamanderman; 25 © Mag. Alban Egger. 31 © R McKown; 33r © Adam Radosavljevic; 34 © Aron Brand; 36 © Stephen Finn; 37 © Rob Ahrens; 42 © Kheng Guan Toh; 52r © oksana.perins; 55 © Joseph Calev.

ISBN 978-0-7627-4921-8

Printed in China
10 9 8 7 6 5 4 3 2 1

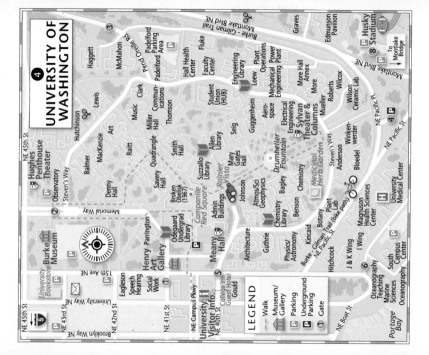